THE
SANDWICH
COOKBOOK

PREPARING FOOD THE HEALTHY WAY SERIES

THE
SANDWICH
COOKBOOK

Frederick E. Kahn, M.D.
Edited by Naomi Silverman

Nautilus Communications, Inc.
New York, N.Y.

The publisher wishes to thank Scott Grayson and Andrea Spirn for their assistance in the preparation of this book.

Published by Nautilus Communications, Inc.
460 East 79th Street, New York, N.Y. 10021

Design by Kathleen Cronin Tinkel

Cover illustration by Marilyn Ackerman

Printed in the United States of America

Contents

Preface

In recent years attention has been focused on the need for each of us to take control of our own future. The concept of self-help means that we should be able to choose how we act in various situations. One of those areas of choice is nutrition—the process or act of nourishing oneself. Furthermore, the changes in the way we feed ourselves have undergone a revolution.

In today's world, we spend time eating and making choices in ways that are very different from our ancestors. Before the use of cooking, people ate raw foods. Eventually, mankind discovered that cooking would change the taste of food. By the Roman times, emphasis was placed on the enjoyment of food as an activity, and as such, more attention was paid to its preparation. As our modes of transportation changed, different cultures were introduced to foods from other areas of the world. Food preparation, however, remained laborious because of all the activities necessary to make food edible. Preservatives were primitive, at best, and packaging was not in use.

With the advent of industrialization, many changes occurred. First of all food could be transported rapidly over long distances. Refrigeration, packaging, and chemistry allowed food to remain for prolonged periods of time on our shelves. Along with these changes, food preparation has also dramatically changed. Instead of using wood, we've moved to gas and electric methods of cooking as well as using microwaves. Food preparation has speeded up in other areas with the advent of tools and machines to cut and process. Agricultural and technological advances have also added another dimension in producing healthier and more bountiful foodstuffs.

The amount of time we have to spend on ourselves is quite different from what our grandparents had. Because of modern conveniences, along with changes in technology, we have much more leisure time. This allows much more time to follow pursuits other than working. Changes in structure of the family have also made us more isolated and the presence of a nuclear-style family, as well as increasing numbers of adult single individuals have promulgated feelings of loneliness. Food, being one of our earliest contacts with our mothers along with feelings of warmth and wholeness, is a direction that we return to when feeling loneliness. Increasing influence of media has also made us also focus much more on different brands of food as well as how and what we are eating. We are aware that we can do something to improve or prolong our lives through exercise and better nutrition.

Social changes have also played an important role in our changing notions of food—and eating. There have been dramatic alterations in the relationship of an individual to those around him or her. Family structure has changed, and where once the large, sprawling family units were the norm, we have now adopted the smaller, tightly knit "nuclear family" style. There are also many more single adults who make up individual households. In both of these situations we are more likely to experience isolation and feelings of loneliness. Psychologists believe that eating is related to the feeling of warmth and security because of their association during infancy. We often eat when feeling lonely, to replace the lost sensation of wholeness that we experience as babies. When we feel this, we may eat too much or eat improperly.

The choice of what and how much food, where and when to eat, and why we are eating, along with an understanding of nutrition, help us develop the essentials of maintaining good health. Coronary heart disease, obesity, dental caries, iron deficiency anemia, and some types of emotional illnesses result from a lack of attention to what we eat. You may significantly improve your health and increase your life span by being actively concerned about your nutritional intake.

This book will offer you a compendium that is directed toward healthier nutrition. It offers recipes which are designed to reduce excesses of foodstuffs that may lead to poor health. It is not a prescription or formula. I take the attitude that there are many different ways to approach life, and as such, the same is true of our eating habits. Thus, this book presents one of these ways in which you can approach the preparation of food—a healthier way!

What you eat, and how you prepare it, is a decision left to each of you. It is your first step toward a more energetic and healthy life.

Frederick E. Kahn, M.D.

Sandwiches

Sandwiches

Legend has it that the sandwich was invented in England by John Montagu, the fourth Earl of Sandwich (1718–92). An avid gambler, he came up with the idea of the sandwich so that he could stay at the gaming tables without interruptions for meals. Montagu, who served as the First Lord of the Admirality, is also said to have been responsible for the decline of the British navy, and his mismanagement of the navy, probably a reason for the British defeat in the American Revolution. Perhaps that is one reason why the food named after him gained such great popularity so quickly in the United States.

Today, the sandwich is the most popular lunch food in the United States. Sandwiches are not only convenient and easy to make, but they can also be tailored to fit anybody's tastes and preferences—no matter how picky or exacting. The variety of food that can be put between two pieces of bread or in the center of a roll is just about endless.

Sandwiches can be made with any kind of bread. They can be eaten as a snack, a main dish, or party fare, depending on how you prepare them. An appetizing light meal can be made of a cold sandwich served with soup, dessert, and a beverage. A hearty meal can be made of hot sandwiches served with juice, salad or a fruit relish, dessert, and a beverage.

Remember, there is no right or wrong way to make a sandwich. If it's edible, tastes good, and fits on or between slices of bread, it's a sandwich!

Sandwich hints

Spread butter lightly on the bread to keep it from absorbing the filling. Cream the butter for easy spreading.

Always choose sandwich fillings that create interesting contrasts in flavor and texture.

Add crisp lettuce, sliced tomatoes, bacon, and similar ingredients to the sandwich at the last minute, since they make the bread soggy and moisten the filling if added early on. For box lunches, wrap these items separately.

When cutting fancy shapes for sandwiches, freeze bread slices for easier cutting and smoother edges.

When sandwiches are prepared ahead of time, cover them with a damp napkin and store them in the refrigerator until served.

Freezing sandwiches

For longer storage, wrap sandwiches in foil, freezer bags, or freezer wrap, and freeze them. They may be wrapped individually, or several sandwiches may be frozen together if separated by freezer paper; this prevents them from sticking together.

Many sandwiches can be frozen for up to two weeks. It is vital to use fresh bread and the freshest ingredients for the filling. Avoid moist spreads that may separate when frozen, such as mayonnaise, salad dressing, or jelly. Use sour cream, applesauce, or milk instead. Never freeze lettuce, onion rings, or tomato slices; add them fresh at serving time.

Different kinds of sandwiches should be wrapped separately to prevent flavors from mingling. Frozen sandwiches thaw in about an hour at room temperature, but will stay fresh for three or four hours after thawing if kept in their wrappings.

Some filling ingredients that freeze well are hard-boiled egg yolks, Roquefort or blue cheese, cream cheese, cheese spread, sliced cheese, sour cream, butter or margarine, canned or cooked chicken, turkey, fish, dried beef, deviled ham, bologna, mild-flavored salami, boiled ham, canned pineapple, applesauce, raisins, peanut butter, prepared mustard, ketchup, chili sauce, and pickles.

Filling ingredients that do not freeze well are hard-boiled egg whites, cottage cheese, cooked bacon, lettuce and other fresh vegetables, apples, preserves, jellies, jams, mayonnaise, and salad dressing.

Breads for sandwiches

The choice of breads to use for sandwiches is as unlimited as your imagination. These are some of the many kinds available.

Loaves

White—sliced or unsliced; round, soft, or firm; French, Italian, Greek, Jewish, Vienna, Irish soda, potato, seeded, or salt-free

Wheat—whole wheat, cracked wheat, oatmeal, graham, protein, gluten, health, or bran

Rye—dark or light; sweet or sour; soft or firm; plain or seeded; sliced, thin-sliced, or unsliced; salty, Swedish, German, Jewish, American, Bavarian, pumpernickel, or raisin pumpernickel

Cornmeal—anadama, salt-rising, onion, honey-flavored, or cheese

Raisin and cinnamon-raisin

Boston brown

Nut, date-nut, or orange-nut

Wreaths and rings

Rolls

White, whole wheat, rye, Italian, French, hard and soft dinner rolls, hamburger and frankfurter buns, finger rolls, long rolls for heros and poorboys, English muffins, crumpets, biscuits, croissants, brioches, bagels, and bialys

Garnishes for sandwiches
orange or grapefruit sections
cucumber sticks
raw zucchini slices
orange cups filled with cranberry sauce
pimento strips
olives—green, ripe, or stuffed
raisins
lemon or lime wedges dipped in chopped parsley or paprika
cauliflowerets
pickled onions
cream-cheese balls rolled in chopped nuts
spiced crabapples
grape jelly in small pear halves
potato chips, corn curls, or chips
cherry tomatoes filled with seasoned cottage cheese
radishes
carrots
celery
green onions
pickled peppers
watercress
curly endive
mint
parsley
apple or pear wedges dipped in lemon juice
grape clusters
stuffed eggs
jellied cranberry-sauce cutouts
chutney or piccalilli
tomato wedges
sweet or dill pickles

Garnishes for open-face sandwiches
chopped hard-boiled eggs
parsley sprigs
paprika
pimento or olive slices
watercress sprigs

Sandwiches for a crowd
Sandwich-making goes faster when you use production-line techniques. First make

the filling. Then line up the bread slices two by two in rows. With a flexible spatula, spread softened butter or margarine to the edges of all the slices. Spread filling on one pair of slices; top with remaining slices; cut and wrap sandwiches. When making more than one type of sandwich, cut and wrap one variety before proceeding to another. Large quantities of sandwiches should be separated with sheets of wax paper, covered with a damp napkin, and stored in the refrigerator until served.

1 medium head of lettuce averages 16 leaves

1 pint of mayonnaise covers about 50 average
   slices of bread if you use 1½ teaspoons (½ tablespoon) per slice

1 pound of softened butter or margarine covers about 96
   slices if you use 1 teaspoon per slice

1 pound of cheese averages 16 slices

WEIGHTS AND MEASURES

dash — slightly less than ¼ teaspoon
3 teaspoons — 1 tablespoon
2 tablespoons — ⅛ cup — 1 ounce
4 tablespoons — ¼ cup — 2 ounces
5 ⅓ tablespoons — ⅓ cup
8 tablespoons — ½ cup — 4 ounces
10 ⅔ tablespoons — ⅔ cup
2 cups — 1 pint — ½ quart — 1 pound
4 cups — 2 pints — 1 quart
4 quarts — 1 gallon
8 dry quarts — 1 peck
4 pecks — 1 bushel

CAN SIZES

8 ounces — 1 cup
12 ounces — 1 ½ cup
1 pound or 16 ounces — 2 cups
20 ounces — 2 ½ cups

ABBREVIATIONS

c.   – cup(s)

env   – envelope(s)

F.   – Fahrenheit

gal.   – gallon(s)

in.   – inch(es)

med.   – medium

min.   – minute(s)

oz.   – ounce(s)

pkg.   – package(s)

pt.   – pint(s)

lb.   – pound(s)

qt.   – quart(s)

sec.   – second(s)

T.   – tablespoon(s)

t.   – teaspoon(s)

Sandwich spreads

Sandwich spreads

Just about all of the spreads in this chapter can be used alone as fillings for simple sandwiches, or they can be combined with other ingredients, such as eggs, fruits, vegetables, meat, seafood, or poultry—in any combination that appeals to you—to make more elaborate sandwiches. You can also invent your own sandwich spreads by experimenting with different kinds of foods you like.

Homemade mayonnaise

Homemade mayonnaise is a bit more yellow and a great deal more flavorful than the store-bought kind. In addition, it is free of chemical preservatives.

2 egg yolks
1 pt. olive oil
1 t. salt
½ t. dry mustard
lemon juice or wine
   vinegar

All ingredients must be
   room temperature.

Beat the egg yolks, salt, and mustard together with a whisk, egg beater, or electric mixer. Add the oil, a few drops at a time, beating the mixture thoroughly after every few drops. If it curdles, you have been adding the oil too quickly. To correct this, separate a third egg and, in a separate bowl, beat the yolk and slowly add a few drops of oil to it; beat it well. Gradually add this beaten egg yolk and oil to your original mixture, beating it very slowly. Continue adding oil a few drops at a time, until your mixture is very thick and stiff. Add a small amount of lemon juice or vinegar to thin out the mixture; beat it in. Taste and add a little more until the taste and thickness is right. Store in a tightly lidded jar in the refrigerator.

Makes 2 cups.

Sandwich butters

Sandwich butters may be used to fill dainty party sandwiches, or on bases of canapés—butter keeps the base from getting soggy. They are also used instead of ordinary butter in making simple sandwiches from sliced meats, poultry, or cheese. Let the butter stand at room temperature until it is soft, but not oily, then cream it with a fork for easy blending.

Green pepper butter

Remove the seeds and membranes from 3 or 4 green peppers. Cook peppers in boiling water until soft; drain well. Finely chop, drain again, and rub through a sieve. Add pulp to ½ cup of softened butter.

Olive butter

Mash ripe or stuffed olives. Mix with an equal amount of softened butter.

Onion butter

Mix ½ cup of finely minced young onions with ½ cup softened butter.

Sandwich spreads

Pimento butter

Drain 3 large pimentos and rub through a sieve. Blend the pulp into ½ cup softened butter. Add salt to taste.

Sardine butter

Remove bones and skins from sardines (or use boneless and skinless variety). Mash well. Blend with an equal amount of softened butter. Add lemon and onion juice to taste.

Shrimp butter

Clean and finely chop 1 pound of cooked or canned shrimp. Blend with 1 cup of softened butter. Purée in electric blender or rub through a sieve.

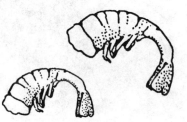

Smoked salmon butter

Finely mince ¼ pound smoked salmon. Mix with 1 cup of softened butter. Add a few drops of lemon juice. Season with white pepper to taste.

Anchovy butter

Mix anchovy paste with an equal amount of softened butter. Add a few drops of onion juice and lemon juice.

Horseradish butter

¼ c. butter
¼ c. grated horseradish
1 t. lemon juice
salt to taste
sugar to taste

Cream butter with all ingredients.

Vegetarian nut butter

¼ lb. almonds
½ lb. pecans
½ lb. hazelnuts or
   filberts
½ lb. roasted peanuts
¼ c. butter

Shell, blanch, and grind the nuts. Knead nuts into butter. Pack tightly in jelly glasses and place in the refrigerator. Before using, dip glass in hot water, so that mixture slips out easily. Cut into slices.

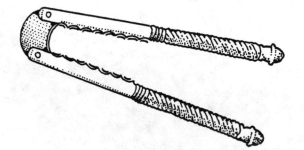

Cheese spreads

Cottage cheese spread

½ c. cottage cheese,
    creamed
cream or milk
¼ c. pimentos or stuffed
    olives, chopped

Blend cheese and a little cream or milk to a smooth paste. Stir in the pimentos. ½ cup chopped walnuts may be added. Add salt to taste.

Blue cheese and nut spread

¼ lb. blue cheese
¼ c. butter, softened
¼ lb. walnut meats,
    chopped
salt and paprika to taste

Crumble the cheese and mix with the butter and nuts. Season with salt and paprika.

Cheddar cheese spread

¾ lb. Cheddar cheese,
    grated
¼ t. salt
paprika
½ t. mustard
1 T. butter

Season cheese with salt, paprika, and mustard. Add butter. Cream and stir until smooth.

Cheddar cheese and anchovy spread

2 T. butter, softened
¼ c. Cheddar cheese,
   grated
1 t. anchovy paste
1 t. vinegar
salt, paprika, and
   mustard to taste

Mix the butter, cheese, anchovy paste, and vinegar. Season.

Potted Cheddar cheese spread

1 T. butter
¼ lb. Cheddar cheese,
   finely cut or grated
⅛ t. cayenne pepper
¼ c. cream
1 egg yolk

Melt the butter in a saucepan. Add cheese and pepper; stir until cheese melts. Add cream to beaten yolk and pour into cheese mixture; cook, stirring constantly, until thick and smooth. Pour into small jars and store in refrigerator.

Roquefort spread

⅛ lb. Roquefort cheese
¼ lb. cream cheese
1 T. butter
1 T. lemon juice
1 t. salt
½ t. chives, finely cut

Mash the cheese. Blend all ingredients until smooth.

Potted snappy cheese spread

1 lb. snappy cheese,
   grated
2 t. salt
1 t. prepared mustard
a few grains of cayenne
½ c. diluted vinegar
1 t. oil

Mix cheese, dry ingredients, and vinegar until blended. Add oil to make a smooth paste. Pack into jars and store in refrigerator.

Camembert spread

½ lb. Camembert cheese
2 T. butter
½ t. paprika
3 or 4 dashes Tabasco
3 drops Worcestershire
   sauce

Blend all ingredients together until smooth.

Camembert-Roquefort spread

½ lb. Camembert cheese
¼ lb. Roquefort cheese
¼ lb. butter
garlic
paprika to taste
parsley, chopped

Mix cheese and butter in a bowl that has been rubbed with garlic. Mold and chill. Unmold, sprinkle with paprika and chopped parsley.

Cream cheese spreads

Cream cheese spreads may be used alone as filling for dainty sandwiches, or in combination with other fillings for lunchbox sandwiches. Sweet cream cheese spreads are popular on fruit, raisin, or nut breads for light meals or snacks, and the savory mixtures also make hearty sandwiches. Soften the cream cheese by letting it stand at room temperature for 30 minutes; then mash with a fork and blend with other ingredients.

Basic cream cheese spread

Mix softened cream cheese with milk, cream (plain or whipped), evaporated milk, or mayonnaise. Beat with a fork until smooth.

Clam and cream cheese spread

1 can minced clams, drained
3 oz. cream cheese, softened
Worcestershire sauce to taste
pinch of dry mustard
salt to taste
onion juice to taste
clam juice

Mix clams and cream cheese. Season with Worcestershire, mustard, salt, and onion juice. If spread is too thick, add clam juice.

Olive cream cheese spread

Mix 8 ounces softened cream cheese and ½ cup drained chopped green olives (stuffed or ripe).

Watercress cream cheese spread

Chop 1 cup of washed watercress. Mix with 8 ounces softened cream cheese.

Watercress and nut cream cheese spread

Chop ½ cup of nuts. Mix well with minced watercress and 8 ounces softened cream cheese.

Sandwich spreads

Pepper-relish cream cheese spread

Mix 8 ounces softened cream cheese and ½ cup drained pepper relish Blend until smooth.

Pimento cream cheese spread

Mix 8 ounces softened cream cheese and ½ cup chopped, drained pimentos.

Pineapple cream cheese spread

Mix 8 ounces softened cream cheese and ½ cup drained, crushed pineapple.

Prune spread

½ lb. cooked prunes,
pitted, drained, and
chopped
2 T. butter, softened
2 (3 oz.) pkg. cream
cheese
¼ c. walnuts, chopped

Blend all ingredients.

Tangy cheese spread

Cream thoroughly equal amounts of cream cheese and butter. Add salt to taste and
paprika. Add 1 teaspoon each of finely minced parsley, capers, pickles, olives, and
green pepper. Flavor with anchovy paste, if you wish.

Seafood spreads

Crab meat spread

2 hard-boiled egg yolks
1 T. butter, melted
1 T. lemon juice
½ lb. canned crab meat,
    finely chopped

Mash the yolks and butter to a smooth paste. Add the lemon juice and the crab meat and mix well.

Salmon spread

1 can (7¾ oz.) salmon,
    drained and flaked
1 hard-boiled egg,
    chopped
2 T. French dressing
2 T. green olives,
    chopped
lemon juice to taste
mayonnaise

Lightly blend all ingredients. Use enough mayonnaise to make a spreadable, but not too moist mixture.

Seafood spread

Chop any cooked seafood. Season with salt, pepper, prepared mustard, and lemon juice, or moisten with any salad dressing.

Tuna fish spread

1 can (6½ or 7 oz.)
   tuna, drained and
   finely flaked
¼ c. celery, minced
½ t. lemon juice
1 T. chili sauce
mayonnaise
salt and pepper to taste

Blend all ingredients. Use just enough mayonnaise to make a spreadable, but not too moist mixture. Season to taste.

Egg and sardine spread

Use equal amounts of hard-cooked egg yolks and sardines (drained, skinned, and boned). Season with salt, cayenne pepper, and mustard. Mash until smooth. Add lemon juice and olive oil to make a paste (mayonnaise can be used instead of lemon juice and oil).

Caviar spread

¼ lb. caviar
2 T. lemon juice
paprika
3 T. olive oil

Blend caviar, lemon juice, a little paprika, and olive oil.

Fruit and vegetable spreads

Cherry and pineapple spread

Pit and slice dark red cherries, then drain. Add an equal amount of crushed pineapple and ¼ cup finely chopped, blanched almonds. Moisten with mayonnaise.

Cucumber spread

Pare and chop a medium cucumber. Season with grated onion. Mix with mayonnaise. 4 hard-boiled eggs, finely chopped, may be added if desired.

Fruit and nut spread

1 lb. raisins or figs
1 lb. dates or prunes
juice of 2 oranges
juice of 2 lemons
½ lb. pecans
½ lb. English walnuts

Remove stems and pits of fruit; finely chop or grind. Moisten with fruit juices. Add finely chopped nuts. Keeps well in the refrigerator in tightly sealed jars.

Mushroom spread

Sauté mushrooms. Cool and chop fine. Season. Mix with mayonnaise.

Avocado or alligator pear spread

Peel and mash a ripe avocado. Season with salt, pepper, and lemon or lime juice. If desired, French dressing or mayonnaise may be added.

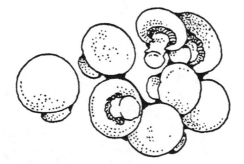

Egg or cheese sandwiches

Egg or cheese sandwiches

Eggs aren't only for breakfast. Cheese isn't married to ham-and-rye. These two common, everyday foods can be turned into a variety of delectable sandwiches.

Egg salad sandwiches

6 hard-boiled eggs,
  finely chopped
½ c. celery, finely
  chopped
¼ c. pickle relish, well
  drained
½ c. mayonnaise
1 t. salt
bread

Mix first 5 ingredients in a bowl. Cover and refrigerate until ready to make the sandwiches. Serve sandwiches at once after they're made, or keep them in the refrigerator.

Variations. For onion-egg sandwiches, use ½ c. of finely chopped green onion instead of the pickle relish.

For egg salad boats, cut off the tops of long sandwich buns and hollow out the inside; fill the hollows with egg salad.

Or, add to egg salad: sliced olives, chopped sardines, diced celery, diced ham, sunflower seeds, or crumbled bacon.

Makes about 2½ cups, or enough for 8 to 10 sandwiches.

Egg and piccalilli sandwiches

⅔ c. hard-boiled eggs,
  chopped
3 T. sweet pickle relish
  or piccalilli
¼ c. mayonnaise or
  salad dressing
8 slices bread
3 T. butter or
  margarine, softened

Combine eggs, piccalilli, and mayonnaise. Spread 3 tablespoons filling between slices of buttered bread.

Makes 4 sandwiches.

Spicy egg salad sandwiches

4 hard-boiled eggs
1½ t. salt
2 T. lemon juice
1 t. Worcestershire sauce
　(optional)
½ t. ground red pepper
　(or black pepper)
⅓ c. mayonnaise
1 slice onion, finely
　chopped
2 stalks celery, finely
　chopped
¼ c. green pepper,
　diced

Mash eggs with a fork in a mixing bowl. Add all other ingredients and stir until well mixed.

Makes 4 sandwiches.

Ham and egg sandwiches

2 t. butter
4 eggs
¼ c. cold water
salt and pepper to taste
¼ lb. boiled ham,
　chopped
6 slices buttered toast

Beat eggs with water, salt, and pepper. Pour eggs into melted butter in a hot skillet. Stir over low heat until set but creamy. Spread ham on toast and cover with eggs. Serve hot.

Makes 3 sandwiches.

Egg or cheese sandwiches

Ham and egg sandwich puffs

2 t. butter
½ c. onions, chopped
¾ c. green peppers,
  chopped
2 c. fresh tomatoes,
  chopped
2 c. cooked ham,
  minced
1 c. Cheddar cheese,
  grated
12 slices white bread
mayonnaise
8 eggs
½ c. evaporated milk
¼ c. water
¼ t. pepper
½ t. salt
½ c. Parmesan cheese,
  grated

Sauté onions, green peppers, tomatoes, and ham in butter; stir over low heat until mixture is reduced. Add cheese and stir until melted. Spread mayonnaise on bread slices. Arrange 6 slices in a buttered 13½x9-in. baking dish. Top each slice with ham mixture and then another slice of bread. Beat eggs, milk, water, and seasonings; pour over sandwiches. Sprinkle grated cheese over sandwiches. Bake for 35—40 min., or until sandwiches are browned and puffed. Cut around sandwiches with a spatula, lift out with surrounding egg custard, and serve.

Makes 6 sandwiches.

Preheat oven to 350° F.

Open-face chutney, egg, and ham sandwiches

4 eggs
½ c. ham
2 T. chutney
2 slices bread, toasted

Mix the eggs, ham, and chutney. Fry in a skillet until set. Place under broiler until mixture is browned and puffy. Serve on toast.

Makes 2 sandwiches.

Western omelet sandwiches

6 eggs
¾ c. milk
½ t. salt
dash of pepper
¾ c. cooked ham,
   minced
⅓ c. onions, minced
⅓ c. green peppers,
   minced
3 T. butter, margarine,
   bacon drippings, or
   shortening
6 frankfurter rolls, split,
   buttered, and toasted

Beat eggs, milk, salt, and pepper in a medium bowl with a wire whisk or hand beater. Add ham, onions, and green pepper. Pour egg mixture into melted butter in a large skillet; cook until set around edges. With spatula, gently lift edges as they set, tilting skillet to allow uncooked portion to run under omelet and shaking occasionally to keep omelet moving freely. When omelet is set but still moist, increase heat slightly to brown bottom. Cut omelet into wedges. Roll each wedge and place in a bun.

Makes 6 sandwiches.

Pancake sandwiches

1 c. flour, sifted
½ t. salt
1 t. baking powder
1 t. sugar
1 c. milk
1 t. salad oil
4 eggs

Sift dry ingredients. Blend milk, oil, and eggs and combine with dry ingredients. Pour batter onto hot greased griddle to make 4-in. pancakes. While pancakes are browning, fry the eggs. Place 1 egg between 2 pancakes. Top with a tablespoon of jam or jelly.

Makes 4 sandwiches.

Egg or cheese sandwiches

Grilled cheese sandwiches

8 slices bread
prepared mustard
butter, softened
4 slices cheese

Spread mustard on 4 slices bread and butter on remaining 4 slices. Put 4 slices of cheese on 4 slices of bread and top with remaining bread. Place sandwiches in a heated, buttered frying pan over medium heat. Fry 1 side until golden, turn with spatula, and fry other side.

Makes 4 sandwiches.

Grilled cheese and bacon sandwiches

2 slices bacon, fried and
   drained
2 slices cheese
2 slices bread

Place a slice of your favorite cheese on a slice of bread. Put the slices of bacon over the cheese. Cover the bacon with the other piece of cheese and bread. In a greased skillet over a medium-low flame, grill 1 side of the sandwich for 2−3 min., until the bread is golden. Turn it over with a spatula and brown the other side.

Makes 1 sandwich.

Puffed cheese sandwiches

1−1¼ c. grated sharp
   cheese (about ⅓ lb.)
1 egg
3 T. milk or cream
a few grains of salt
½ t. paprika
8 slices bread

Beat eggs well. Blend in milk, salt, and paprika. Add the cheese and beat thoroughly with a fork. Toast the bread slices on one side only; spread the cheese mixture on the untoasted sides. Place the sandwiches under the broiler until the cheese is puffed up and slightly browned. Serve very hot.

Makes 4 sandwiches.

THE SANDWICH COOKBOOK

Cheddar and egg sandwiches

2 hard-boiled eggs,
  chopped
½ c. walnuts, chopped
1 c. Cheddar cheese,
  grated
3 T. mayonnaise

Mix all ingredients. Spread on bread or crackers. Broil to melt cheese or serve cold without melting cheese.

Makes 4 servings.

Broiled cheese-and-olive sandwiches

1 c. ripe olives, chopped
½ c. green onions,
  slivered
1½ c. Cheddar cheese,
  grated
½ c. mayonnaise
½ t. salt
½ t. curry or chili
  powder
6 English muffins, split
  and toasted

Combine first 6 ingredients and spread on muffins. Broil until cheese melts.

Makes 3 servings.

Bacon-chili-cheese sandwiches

2 c. sharp American
  cheese, shredded
  (½ lb.)
½ c. green pepper,
  finely diced
6 slices bacon, cooked
  and diced
6 T. chili sauce
½ t. Worcestershire
  sauce
6–8 buttered rolls or
  buns, or 12–16 slices
  bread

Mix all ingredients and spread generously on buttered rolls, buns, or thick slices of French bread. Place on a baking sheet in 425° F. oven until lightly browned.

Makes 3 cups of spread, enough for 6–8 sandwiches.

Egg or cheese sandwiches

Denver omelet sandwiches

4 eggs
¼ c. milk
dash of pepper
1 pkg. (2½ oz.) thinly
   sliced smoked ham,
   chopped
¼ c. celery
2 t. butter
4 slices Vienna bread,
   ½-in. thick, toasted
   and buttered
4 slices (1 oz. each)
   Colby cheese, halved
   diagonally
4 slices tomato

Beat eggs, milk, and pepper, then stir in ham and celery. Heat 2 teaspoons butter in a skillet and cook egg mixture like scrambled eggs. Divide egg mixture evenly on slices of toasted bread. Top eggs with 2 cheese triangles and 1 slice tomato. Broil until cheese melts.

Makes 4 sandwiches.

Baked ham-egg-Swiss cheese sandwiches

6 slices white bread,
   toasted and buttered
6 (¼-in.) slices cooked
   tender ham
6 (⅛-in.) slices Swiss
   cheese
6 slices tomato
salt and pepper to taste
6 eggs, poached
12 strips pimento

Place toast in a low casserole or baking pan. Cover with ham and cheese. Cook in 400° F. oven until cheese melts. Top with slice of tomato; dust lightly with a little salt and pepper; finish with 1 poached egg. Top with crisscrossed strips of pimento. Serve immediately.

Makes 6 sandwiches.

Asparagus-cheese sandwich soufflés

6 slices white bread,
   toasted and buttered
12 slices tomato
6 slices sharp processed
   American cheese
asparagus spears,
   cooked
3 egg yolks
salt and pepper to taste
1 T. French salad
   dressing
3 egg whites, stiffly
   beaten

Place toast with buttered side up on baking sheet. Top each slice with 2 slices tomato, 1 slice cheese, and a few asparagus spears. Beat egg yolks until thick; add salt, pepper, and French dressing. Fold into beaten egg whites; spoon over asparagus. Bake at 350° F. for 15 min., or until egg mixture is lightly browned.

Makes 6 sandwiches.

Brick cheese and ham sandwiches

Place a slice of brick cheese on a slice of bread. Cover with thinly sliced sweet-sour pickles and a slice of ham. Top with another slice of bread.

Brick cheese and tomato sandwiches

Place a slice of brick cheese on a slice of bread. Cover with slices of tomato and chopped green pepper. Top with another slice of bread.

Sweetbread and cheese sandwiches

Place slices of cooked sweetbread between slices of Cheddar cheese in a sandwich.

Tortilla sandwiches

2 flour tortillas
½ c. refried beans
¼ c. Cheddar cheese,
  shredded
¼ c. lettuce, shredded
¼ c. tomato, chopped
2 T. sour cream

Fill tortillas with ingredients in the order given. Fold ends of tortillas and roll up.

Makes 2 sandwiches.

Fruit and vegetable sandwiches

Fruit and vegetable sandwiches

Sliced, chopped, or mashed, hot or cold, cooked or raw—these are some of the many ways fruits and vegetables can be used in sandwiches. The recipes in this chapter just hint at the possibilities. Use your imagination to create sumptuous sandwiches from these health-giving foods.

Lettuce sandwiches

Wash and dry fresh, crisp lettuce leaves. Place them between thin slices of buttered bread; spread with mayonnaise.

Onion sandwiches

Cut Bermuda onions into thin slices; sprinkle with salt and a few grains of sugar. Place between slices of rye bread that have been buttered or spread with goose fat or chicken fat. Or fry the onions in fat until tender, then add salt and pepper and serve on a slice of fresh or toasted rye bread.

Raisin-coconut-yogurt sandwiches

½ c. plain yogurt
½ c. unsweetened
  shredded coconut
½ c. raisins

Mix all ingredients in a bowl. Spread on toast or bread.

Makes 3—4 sandwiches.

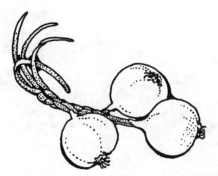

Pineapple-pecan-cream cheese sandwiches

1 pkg. (3 oz.) cream
  cheese
¼ c. crushed pineapple,
  well drained
¼ c. pecans, chopped

Mix cheese, pineapple, and pecans. Spread on wheat bread.

Makes 1—2 sandwiches.

Raisin-nut-cream cheese sandwiches

1½ c. raisins
1 pkg. (3 oz.) cream
  cheese
½ c. peanut butter
1 t. honey, if desired
¼ c. walnuts, chopped
4 slices nut, banana, or
  apricot bread

Soak raisins in hot water for 10 min. Drain and chop. Mix with cream cheese, peanut butter, honey, and walnuts. Spread between slices of bread.

Makes 2 sandwiches.

Walnut-apple-cream cheese sandwiches

¼ c. cream cheese
2 T. walnuts, chopped
2 T. celery, chopped
3 T. apple, chopped
1 t. cinnamon
4 slices raisin bread

Mix cream cheese, walnuts, celery, apple, and cinnamon. Spread between two slices of raisin bread.

Makes 2 sandwiches.

Strawberry-cream cheese sandwiches

¼ c. cream cheese,
  softened
2 T. strawberry
  preserves
1 T. wheat germ
2 slices whole wheat
  bread

Mix cheese, preserves, and wheat germ. Spread between bread slices. Cut in half or quarters.

Makes 1 sandwich.

Fried banana sandwiches

1 firm, slightly green
  banana per person
1 T. butter or margarine
  per panful

Slice the peeled banana on an angle into ½-in. pieces. Melt the butter in a saucepan over a low flame. Fry the banana pieces until they are lightly browned, turning occasionally. Serve warm between slices of plain bread or bread spread with cream cheese, sour cream, honey, jam, or any combination of these.

Meat sandwiches

Meat sandwiches

Do you ever get an intense craving for corned beef on rye with mustard and a pickle? Or baked Virginia ham on a roll? Sandwiches like these are practically American institutions. In this chapter, you'll find recipes for some old favorites as well as new ideas for making sandwiches from the meats we love to eat.

Reuben sandwiches

rye bread
nd
dressing
12 slices Swiss cheese
½ c. sauerkraut
24 slices corned beef
butter

Spread dressing on one side of 12 slices of bread. Place a slice of cheese, 2 teaspoons sauerkraut, and 2 slices of corned beef on each of the 12 slices of bread. Stack 2 of these slices and top with a plain slice of bread. Hold sandwiches together with toothpicks. Butter outside of bread and grill sandwiches until cheese melts.

Makes 6 sandwiches.

Corned beef in rolls

4 hard-boiled eggs,
  coarsely chopped
½ c. celery, diced
1 green onion, finely
  sliced
¼ c. mayonnaise
2 t. prepared mustard
2 T. sweet-pickle relish,
  drained
¼ t. salt
1 can (12 oz.) corned
  beef, sliced and
  chilled
6 sandwich rolls,
  buttered
lettuce leaves

Combine eggs, celery, and onion. Mix mayonnaise, mustard, pickle relish, and salt; mix into egg mixture. Place corned beef slices on bottom half of roll and top with egg-mayonnaise mixture. Follow with lettuce and top half of roll.

Makes 6 sandwiches.

Roast beef on rye sandwiches

½ c. sour cream
1 T. dry onion soup mix
1 t. horseradish, drained
¼ t. salt
dash of pepper
12 slices cold roast beef
8 slices rye bread,
   buttered
4 lettuce leaves
4 slices garlic dill pickle

Mix first 5 ingredients. Place 3 slices of beef on 4 bread slices; top with lettuce leaf, a spoonful of sour-cream mixture, and a second bread slice. Cut diagonally. Serve with a garnish of dill pickle.

Makes 4 sandwiches.

Beef stroganoff sandwiches

1 T. chopped onions
1 T. butter
1 can (10½ oz.)
   mushroom gravy or 1
   can (10¾ oz.) beef
   gravy
½ c. sour cream
1 T. dry white wine
pinch dried basil,
   crushed
6 slices roast beef
6 slices toast

Sauté onions in butter until limp but not brown. Mix in gravy, sour cream, wine, and basil. Add beef. Heat through, stirring occasionally, for 5—7 min. Serve over hot toast.

Makes 6 sandwiches.

French-toasted ham sandwiches

½ lb. cold boiled ham,
  finely chopped or
  ground
prepared English
  mustard
8 thin slices day-old
  bread
2 eggs
¾ c. milk
2 T. butter

Moisten ham with mustard and spread between bread
slices; press firmly together. Beat eggs slightly, add
milk, and beat again. Dip sandwich in egg mixture
and sauté in butter until golden on both sides. Should
be eaten with a knife and fork.

Makes 4 sandwiches.

Ham or smoked beef sandwiches

½ lb. cold boiled ham
  or smoked pickled
  beef
¼ c. mayonnaise
thin slices of bread

Chop the ham or smoked beef very finely. Mix well
with mayonnaise. Spread on bread.

Makes 2 sandwiches.

Ham salad sandwiches

2 c. cooked ham
½ c. sweet pickles or
  pickle relish, drained
2 hard-boiled eggs,
  chopped
½ c. celery, finely
  chopped
½ c. mayonnaise or
  salad dressing
1 t. prepared mustard
bread

Dice ham and pickles in food chopper or processor. In
a small bowl, mix the ham-pickle mixture with
chopped eggs, celery, mayonnaise, and mustard.
Refrigerate until needed. Spread on slices of white or
whole wheat bread. Top with a lettuce leaf.

Makes 6–8 sandwiches.

Fancy Canadian bacon sandwiches

1 c. canned pineapple
juice
3 T. prepared mustard
½ c. brown sugar,
packed
1 T. prepared
horseradish
18 (1 oz.) slices
Canadian bacon
24 canned French-fried
onion rings, heated
12 slices wheat bread

Mix pineapple juice, mustard, sugar, and horseradish. Add Canadian bacon slices and let marinate for at least 2 hours. Remove bacon from sauce and brown bacon on both sides under moderately hot broiler. Place 3 slices bacon and 4 onion rings between each 2 bread slices.

Makes 6 sandwiches.

Open-face BLT sandwiches

6 large slices rye bread,
buttered
3 c. lettuce, finely
shredded
3 tomatoes, thinly sliced
1 c. bottled creamy blue-
cheese salad dressing
12 slices bacon, crisply
cooked
12 black olives, pitted

Top each slice of bread with lettuce and 3 or 4 tomato slices. Cover with dressing and top with bacon and olives.

Variation. For avocado BLT sandwiches, add avocado slices to sandwiches and serve open-face with Thousand Island dressing.

Open-face pepper-steak sandwiches

1½ lb. top-round beef
  steak, ½-in. thick
unseasoned instant meat
  tenderizer
butter or margarine
2 med. green peppers,
  cut into thin strips
1 pkg. (1 oz.) brown
  gravy-seasoning mix
1 c. water
1 loaf Italian bread,
  about 12-in. long
½ t. garlic salt
½ t. basil (optional)

Sprinkle steak with tenderizer as label directs and cut into ½-in. strips. In a large skillet over high heat, melt 2 tablespoons butter and fry meat for 3 min., stirring occasionally. Stir in peppers, gravy-seasoning mix, and 1 cup water. Cook for another 5 min., or until meat is tender, stirring occasionally. Cut bread in half horizontally; spread with butter and sprinkle with garlic salt and basil. Broil bread halves until toasted. Spoon meat mixture over bread halves. Cut each half into thirds.

Makes 6 sandwiches.

Preheat broiler.

Veal-and-mozzarella sandwiches

1 stick butter
1 t. anchovy paste, or 2
  anchovy fillets,
  mashed
1 t. dry mustard
1 t. oregano
12 thin slices white
  bread, crusts
  removed, toasted on
  1 side
12 thin slices veal, 2x2-
  in., cooked
12 thin slices mozzarella
  cheese, 2x2-in.

Cream butter, anchovy paste, mustard, and oregano. Spread on untoasted side of bread slices and top with veal and then cheese. Broil at low heat until cheese melts.

Makes 6 sandwiches.

Liver paste sandwiches

½ lb. cooked liver
  (calf's, steer, pork,
  chicken, or goose)
½ c. poultry fat
2 hard-boiled eggs
½ onion, grated
½ t. salt
⅛ t. pepper
bread

Sauté liver in ¼ cup of the fat until cooked through, or bake in moderate oven. Grind first 5 ingredients in a meat grinder several times until very fine, or purée in an electric blender. Add remaining fat to make a light paste. Spread on bread.

Makes 4 sandwiches.

Liver paste and mushroom sandwiches

½ lb. raw liver, sliced
2 T. chicken fat,
  rendered
½ c. mushrooms, finely
  chopped
lemon juice
onion juice
salt and pepper to taste
bread

Sauté liver in fat until tender, then grind. Sauté mushrooms in fat. Mix liver and mushrooms and add seasonings. Add more fat if necessary to make a smooth paste.

Makes 4 sandwiches.

Mock pâté de foie gras sandwiches

Remove casing from liver sausage. Mash to a paste with mayonnaise. Spread between thin slices of buttered rye bread.

Sweetbread sandwiches

Chop cold, cooked sweetbreads. Mix with mayonnaise, chopped celery, and nut meats.

Chicken liver pâté and brisket of beef sandwiches

Spread butter and plenty of chicken liver pâté on thin slices of sour-rye bread. Top with thinly sliced brisket (fat removed). Garnish with whole cherry tomatoes and watercress.

Foie gras sandwiches

Slice whole foie gras or use pâté de foie gras. Top sandwiches with thinly sliced cucumber or tomato.

Peanut butter sandwiches

Peanut butter sandwiches

You could fill a whole cookbook with different recipes for peanut butter sandwiches and still have some left over. As you'll see when you try some of these recipes in this chapter, peanut butter does not deserve its lowly reputation. And don't let anybody tell you it's just kid's stuff!

Homemade peanut butter

¼ c. peanut oil
2 c. peanuts
1 T. salt
2 T. honey

Blend all ingredients in a blender. Add more peanuts, if necessary.

Variations. Add to peanut butter: chopped hard-boiled eggs, raisins, chopped banana, shredded carrot, chopped apple, crushed pineapple, grated cheese, sesame seed and celery, raisins and sunflower seed, chopped nuts and coconut, or chopped pears.

Makes 2 cups.

Peanut butter and honey sandwiches

Spread peanut butter and a little honey between slices of white bread. Butter the sandwich on the outside and brown on both sides in a skillet.

Peanut butter and jelly sandwiches

Spread peanut butter and cherry jam or jelly between slices of whole wheat or white bread.

THE SANDWICH COOKBOOK

Peanut butter, bacon, and apple sandwiches

Spread peanut butter between slices of white bread. Top with cooked, crumbled bacon and thin apple slices.

Peanut butter and egg salad sandwiches

4 T. peanut butter
2 hard-boiled eggs,
   finely chopped
2 T. celery, minced
2 T. mayonnaise
½ t. salt
¼ t. prepared mustard
pinch black pepper

Mix all ingredients well. Spread on bread.

Makes 2 sandwiches.

Peanut butter and cheese-olive sandwiches

Spread 1 slice of bread with softened cream cheese. Add a layer of thinly sliced stuffed or pitted olives. Spread another slice of bread with peanut butter. Put slices together.

Makes 1 sandwich.

Peanut butter and marshmallow-cream sandwiches

Spread 1 slice of bread with 1 tablespoon marshmallow cream and then sprinkle with coarsely chopped Spanish peanuts. Spread another slice of bread with creamy peanut butter. Put slices together.

Makes 1 sandwich.

Peanut butter and cranberry sauce sandwiches

Spread 1 slice of bread with jellied cranberry sauce and top with lettuce leaf. Spread another slice with peanut butter. Put slices together.

Makes 1 sandwich.

Peanut butter and coleslaw sandwiches

2 c. cabbage, finely
   shredded
2 T. pimento, diced
2 T. mayonnaise
1 t. wine vinegar
½ t. salt
¼ t. sugar
bread

Toss all ingredients together. Refrigerate about an hour, tossing occasionally. Spread on bread.

Makes 4 sandwiches.

Peanut butter and tuna sandwiches

1 can (7 oz.) tuna, well
   drained
½ c. green pepper,
   minced
2 t. mayonnaise
½ t. salt
½ t. lemon juice
½ t. instant minced
   onion

Mix all ingredients well.

Makes 4 sandwiches.

Peanut butter and date-nut sandwiches

½ c. dates, diced and
   pitted
¼ c. pecans, chopped
bread
peanut butter

Mix dates and pecans and spread on 4 peanut butter
sandwiches.

Makes 4 sandwiches.

Peanut butter and Canadian bacon sandwiches

Arrange 2 slices of cooked Canadian bacon on 1 bread slice; sprinkle with chopped
parsley. Spread another bread slice with peanut butter. Put slices together.

Makes 1 sandwich.

Peanut butter and banana sandwiches

Spread peanut butter on 2 slices of bread. Place thinly sliced banana in between slices.

Makes 1 sandwich.

Peanut butter-carrot-raisin sandwiches

Spread 1 slice of bread with peanut butter and top with 3 or 4 tablespoons grated carrots and 1 tablespoon seedless raisins. Top with another bread slice.

Makes 1 sandwich.

Peanut butter and cucumber sandwiches

Spread 1 slice of bread with peanut butter, sprinkle with 1 tablespoon minced green pepper, and top with 5 thin cucumber slices. Cover with another bread slice.

Makes 1 sandwich.

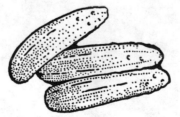

Toasted peanut butter and raisin sandwiches

Spread peanut butter on 2 slices of toast and sprinkle with raisins. Stick slices together.

Makes 1 sandwich.

Toasted peanut butter and banana sandwiches

Spread peanut butter on toast and cover it with sliced banana. Top with another slice of bread.

Makes 1 sandwich.

Peanut butter pizza

½ c. peanut butter
4 English muffin halves
8 slices bacon, cooked,
   drained, and
   crumbled

Spread peanut butter on muffin halves. Top with crumbled bacon. Broil until peanut butter is bubbly.

Makes 2—4 servings.

Grilled peanut butter and banana sandwiches

8 slices bread (white,
    raisin, or whole
    wheat)
peanut butter
2 bananas, peeled and
    sliced
4 eggs
½ c. milk
¼ t. salt
2 T. butter

Spread peanut butter on bread slices according to taste. Arrange banana slices on 4 of the bread slices and top with the 4 remaining slices (with the peanut butter side inside). Beat the eggs, milk, and salt with a fork or rotary beater until mixed well. Pour the egg mixture into a pie pan or plate. In a skillet or griddle over medium heat (325° F. for an electric skillet) melt the butter. Dip the sandwiches, one at a time, into the egg mixture so that both sides have an even yellow coating. Cook each sandwich in the skillet or on the griddle until browned on both sides.

Makes 4 sandwiches.

Applesauce and peanut butter sandwiches

¼ c. peanut butter
¼ c. applesauce
2 dried apricots,
    chopped
¼ c. cottage cheese or
    ricotta cheese
4 slices whole wheat
    toast

Mix first 4 ingredients. Spread on 2 toast slices. Top with remaining toast slices.

Makes 2 sandwiches.

Poultry sandwiches

Poultry sandwiches

Poultry is one of our most versatile foods. Sliced thin, stacked on bread or a roll, and served with a garnish or two, it makes an elegant sandwich. A hot, open-face sandwich with gravy and potatoes will satisfy the heartiest appetite. Whether it is used alone or combined with other ingredients, poultry ranks high in popularity as a sandwich food.

Chicken almond sandwiches

½ c. slivered almonds,
    toasted
½ c. sour cream
2 t. fresh lemon juice
¼ t. ground ginger
¼ t. salt
1½ c. cooked chicken,
    diced
⅔ c. celery, chopped
1 can (8 oz.) crushed
    pineapple, well
    drained
12 slices whole wheat or
    oatmeal bread
butter
lettuce

Coarsely chop nuts in a blender for 10–15 seconds; pour into a small mixing bowl. Blend sour cream, lemon juice, ginger, and salt in the blender for 10 seconds. Add to nuts. Stir in chicken, celery, and pineapple. Chill, covered, for 1–2 hours. Before serving, butter 1 side of each slice of bread. Cover 6 slices with lettuce and spread chicken mixture over lettuce. Top each with a second slice of bread, buttered side facing down.

Makes 6 sandwiches.

Chutney-chicken sandwiches

Spread chopped, drained chutney on slices of buttered white or cheese bread. Put together with thin slices of lightly seasoned chicken.

Creamed chicken on toast

½ boneless chicken
    breast, sliced
1½ T. peanut oil
½ c. water
½ t. salt
¼ t. pepper
1 t. flour
2 pieces of toast

Cook the chicken in hot oil in a medium frying pan over medium heat; stir often. The meat will turn completely white in 2–3 min. Add ½ cup water and cook for 2 min. Stir in salt and pepper. Stir flour into the sauce with a fork for about 1 min., until thickened. Serve over toast.

Makes 2 sandwiches.

Roquefort chicken sandwich

Butter 2 slices of white bread and trim off crusts. Place 1 slice of white chicken meat on 1 slice of bread and sprinkle with Roquefort cheese and paprika. Cover with the other bread slice. Toast on both sides. Garnish with parsley. Serve hot.

Makes 1 sandwich.

Goose meat sandwiches

Spread goose fat on thin slices of fresh or toasted rye bread or rolls. Top with sliced cooked goose. Or, mince the meat, add 1 or 2 pickles, or a little ketchup, and use as filling.

Variation. Use slices of cold duck instead.

Toasted turkey-bacon-cheese sandwiches

4 T. butter or margarine
4 T. flour
¾ t. salt
¼ t. prepared mustard
dash of cayenne pepper
2 c. milk
2 c. grated processed American cheese (½ lb.)
4 slices toast
8 med. slices cooked turkey
¼ t. paprika
4 slices crisp bacon
2 med. tomatoes, sliced

Melt butter in a saucepan over low heat and stir in flour, salt, mustard, and cayenne. Stir in milk and cook until thickened and boiling. Remove from heat and add cheese; stir until melted, making a sauce. Arrange toast in shallow 10x6-in. baking dish. Top each slice with 2 slices of turkey and cheese sauce. Dust with paprika. Bake for 10 min. at 450° F. Garnish with crisp bacon slices and tomato slices.

Makes 4 sandwiches.

Hot turkey sandwiches

1 small can deviled ham
4 slices bread, toasted
8 slices cooked turkey
1 can (10½ oz.)
    condensed mushroom
    soup
3 T. mayonnaise
¼ c. dry sherry
paprika

Spread ham on toast and top with turkey. Place in shallow baking pan. Bring soup, mayonnaise, and sherry to a boil. Spoon sauce over sandwiches. Bake in oven at 400° F. for 10 min. Sprinkle with paprika and serve at once.

Makes 4 sandwiches.

Seafood sandwiches

Seafood sandwiches

The sea offers us an appetizing choice of sandwich fillings—from simple tuna to sophisticated shrimp. Enjoy seafood sandwiches by following the recipes in this chapter, and then make up some of your own.

pen-face Alaska king crab and Swiss cheese sandwiches

1 pkg. (6 oz.) frozen
   Alaska king crab
   meat, defrosted and
   flaked
⅓ c. Italian salad
   dressing (not sweet)
8 large slices rye bread
¼ c. butter, at room
   temperature
4 (1 oz.) slices Swiss
   cheese
8 thin slices tomato
½ c. sour cream
2 T. fresh dill, chopped
   or 1 t. ground dill
   weed
6 lettuce leaves
8 cherry tomatoes
4 lemon wedges

Stir Italian dressing into crab meat; refrigerate for at
least 15 min. Spread butter on bread and cover 4 of the
slices with Swiss cheese and top with crab meat. Cover
each of remaining 4 slices of bread with 2 slices
tomato. Mix sour cream and dill; place a lettuce leaf
filled with 2 tablespoons of this mixture atop each
tomato slice. Arrange 1 of each type of sandwich on
individual plates. Garnish with cherry tomatoes and
lemon wedges.

Makes 8 sandwiches.

Broiled tuna patties

1 can (6½ or 7 oz.)
   tuna, flaked
2 T. onions, chopped
2 T. sweet pickle,
   chopped
¼ c. mayonnaise or
   salad dressing
5 hamburger buns, split
   and toasted
butter
5 slices sharp processed
   American cheese

Mix tuna, onions, pickle, and mayonnaise. Butter
bottom halves of hamburger buns and spread with tuna
mixture. Top each with a slice of cheese. Broil 5-in.
from heat for 4 min. or until cheese melts. Add tops of
buns.

Makes 5 sandwiches.

French-toasted shrimp sandwich

1 lb. shrimp, cooked and
   chopped (about 2 c.)
⅔ c. chili sauce
⅔ c. mayonnaise or
   salad dressing
18 slices bacon, crisply
   cooked
12 slices white bread
½ c. cream cheese,
   softened
3 eggs, beaten
3 t. milk
¾ t. salt
6 parsley sprigs
12 ripe olives
6 sweet pickle fans

Marinate shrimp in chili sauce for 30 min.; then add mayonnaise. Crumble 6 bacon slices into shrimp mixture and toss lightly. Spread bread with cream cheese. Cover 6 slices with shrimp mixture; close sandwiches. Blend eggs, milk, and salt. Heat butter in grill or frying pan. Dip both sides of sandwiches in egg mixture, then grill on both sides until golden. Place 2 bacon slices diagonally across each sandwich; garnish with parsley, 2 olives, 1 pickle fan.

Makes 6 sandwiches.

Lobster sandwiches

6 oz. canned lobster or
   other seafood, flaked
1 t. lemon juice
½ c. celery, minced
1 T. onions or chives,
   minced
½ c. mayonnaise
rye bread, buttered

Sprinkle lemon juice over lobster. Add celery, onions or chives, and mayonnaise. If mayonnaise is too thick, thin it with sour cream. Season with Worcestershire sauce, curry powder, or freshly grated nutmeg, if desired, and add capers, chopped olives, pickles, or parsley. Spread mixture on bread. Top with crisp lettuce leaves, if desired.

Makes 4 sandwiches.

Toasted salmon sandwiches

⅓ c. butter or
  margarine, melted
12 slices white bread
1 can (16 oz.) salmon
1 pkg. (10 oz.) frozen
  peas, cooked and
  drained
¼ c. instant minced
  onion
1 can (10½ oz.)
  condensed cream of
  mushroom soup
4 eggs
2 c. milk

Brush butter on 1 side of each bread slice. Arrange 6 slices, buttered side up, in single layer in a buttered 13x9-in. baking dish. In a bowl, flake salmon with a fork. Stir in peas and onion. Spread mixture evenly over bread slices in baking dish. Cover with remaining bread slices, buttered side up. In another bowl, beat undiluted soup, eggs, and milk with a hand beater until well blended; pour over bread. Bake for 1 hour, or until a knife inserted in custard comes out clean. Serve at once.

Makes 6 servings.

Preheat oven to 325° F.

Olive and sardine sandwiches

1 can (4 oz.) sardines
  in oil, drained
1 hard-boiled egg,
  mashed
6 pimento-stuffed olives,
  mashed
salt, paprika, and lemon
  juice to taste
mayonnaise to moisten
8 slices light rye bread

Mix all ingredients except bread. Spread between bread slices.

Makes 4 sandwiches.

Sweet-tooth sandwiches

Sweet-tooth sandwiches

Sandwiches for dessert? Why not?

Strawberry blintz sandwiches

1½ c. creamed cottage
  cheese
4 eggs
2 T. sugar
12 slices white bread
2 (10 oz.) pkg. frozen
  strawberries in quick-
  thaw pouch
⅓ c. milk
butter or margarine

Beat cottage cheese, 1 egg, and sugar until well mixed. Spread ¼ cup of mixture on each of 6 bread slices; top with remaining slices. Thaw strawberries following label directions. In a pie plate, beat 3 eggs and milk with a fork. In a large skillet over medium-high heat, melt a little butter or margarine. Dip sandwiches, 1 at a time, into egg mixture, coating both sides. Brown both sides in the skillet; place on a warm platter while frying remaining sandwiches. Top with berries.

Makes 6 sandwiches.

Ice-cream sandwiches

1 pt. coffee or vanilla ice
  cream, slightly
  softened
24 large chocolate
  cookies or 24 graham
  crackers

Place 6 cookies in a row on a cookie sheet. Spread ice cream over each cookie and top with a cookie; place in refrigerator or freezer. Make a second batch of 6. These can be kept in the refrigerator for about 15 min. without melting. Store the sandwiches in the freezer for longer periods.

Makes 12 sandwiches.

Ginger jam sandwiches

butter or margarine,
  softened
1 loaf sliced white
  sandwich bread,
  crusts removed
¼ c. crystallized (or
  preserved) ginger
¾ c. orange marmalade

Butter 1 side of each slice of bread. Mix the ginger and marmalade. Spread a thin layer of the mixture on the buttered side of half the slices. Top them with the remaining buttered bread slices.

Makes about 8 sandwiches.

Burgers

Burgers

Chopped meat is like the basic black dress in a woman's wardrobe—you can dress it up or dress it down to suit any occasion. Patties, meatballs, loaves, sauces— anything you can cook with hamburger meat can be served as a sandwich. There is almost no end to the possibilities.

Hamburger hints

Spice up any ground beef recipe with one or more of the following: Worcestershire sauce, chopped onions, chopped green peppers, soy sauce and ginger, mustard, ketchup, pickle relish, barbecue sauce, or prepared horseradish. Add before forming patties.

Hamburger pockets

1 lb. ground beef
4 slices tomato
4 thin slices onion
4 slices Cheddar cheese
salt and pepper to taste
bread

Place beef in a large bowl and mix in salt and pepper with your hands. Place each slice of tomato atop a slice of onion and a slice of cheese. Form 4 patties around the cheese, tomato, and onion; make sure none of the filling ingredients show. Pat the burgers between your hands to make sure that the meat is firmly around the filling. Cook on an outdoor grill or on top of the stove in a heavy frying pan. Turn several times. Serve on homemade rolls or bread instead of the standard packaged hamburger rolls.

Makes 4 burgers.

Broiled hamburger sandwiches

1 lb. ground beef
1 t. salt
¼ t. paprika
2 T. butter or margarine
¼ c. onions, chopped
8 slices bread
butter

Place beef, salt, and paprika in a bowl. Melt butter in a small skillet and sauté onions until they are light yellow; add them to the meat and stir lightly. Reduce oven heat to 350° F. and toast the bread on 1 side about 3-in. from the heat. Spread the toasted sides with the meat mixture; dot tops with butter. Broil the sandwiches about 3-in. from the heat for 5 min., leaving the broiler door partly open. Serve with or without gravy.

Heat oven to 550° F. for
   10 min.

Makes 4 burgers.

Sloppy Joes

2 lb. ground beef
1 T. oil
1 c. onions, peeled and chopped
1 clove garlic, mashed
2 (3 oz.) cans chopped mushrooms, drained
2 (10¾ oz.) cans condensed tomato soup
2 T. prepared mustard
½ t. salt
⅛ t. pepper
12 buns, split and toasted

Brown beef in oil. Add onions and garlic and cook until tender. Stir to separate the pieces of meat; pour off any fat. Add mushrooms, soup, mustard, and seasonings. Simmer over low heat for 10 min., stirring occasionally. Spoon over buns.

Makes 12 burgers.

Blue cheese burgers

2 lb. ground beef
⅓ c. onions, chopped
⅓ c. blue cheese, crumbled
2 t. salt
1 T. Worcestershire sauce
1 loaf French bread
½ c. butter, softened
¼ c. prepared mustard

Combine first 5 ingredients and shape into 10 patties. Cut bread in twenty ½-in. slices. Blend butter and mustard and spread generously on 1 side of each bread slice. Reassemble loaf, buttered sides together. Wrap in heavy foil and place on grill for 15 min. Broil burgers for 8 min.; turn and broil for 4—7 min. Serve between French bread slices.

Makes 10 burgers.

Bacon burgers

6 slices bacon, partially
   cooked
2 lb. ground beef
¼ c. lemon juice
2 t. Worcestershire sauce
salt and pepper to taste
8 buns, toasted

In a wire broiler basket, arrange half the bacon slices side by side. On wax paper, pat the beef into a 12x8-in. rectangle. Combine lemon juice and Worcestershire sauce and brush half over meat. Sprinkle with a little salt and pepper. Carefully turn meat onto bacon in basket; remove wax paper. Brush top with remaining lemon mixture and season with salt and pepper. Lay remaining bacon over top. Close basket and broil on grill over hot coals, turning often, for 20—25 min. or until done. Cut rectangle in 8 squares and serve each in a toasted hamburger bun.

Makes 8 burgers.

Broiled deviled burgers

¼ c. ketchup
2 t. prepared
   horseradish
2 t. onions, finely
   chopped
1½ t. prepared mustard
1½ t. Worcestershire
   sauce
¾ t. salt
dash pepper
1 lb. ground beef
6 hamburger buns, split

Combine first 7 ingredients, then mix in beef. Toast uncut surfaces of buns under broiler. Spread cut sides with beef mixture and broil 3-in. from heat for 6 min.

Makes 6 burgers.

Potato chip burgers

1 egg, beaten
1 lb. ground beef
2 T. onions, finely
   chopped
¼ t. salt
dash pepper
2 T. water
6 c. potato chips (4
   oz.), crushed (2 c.)
4 buns

Mix first 6 ingredients. Stir in chips. Shape into 4 patties. Cook over medium heat for 5 min. on each side. Serve on rolls.

Makes 4 burgers.

Popeye spinach burgers

Use any vegetable to enrich your burgers. Sneaky—but it works!

1 c. spinach (or green
   beans, peas, etc.)
1 lb. ground beef
4 buns

Steam the vegetable and purée in a blender. Mix into ground beef. Form patties and broil. Serve with or without buns.

Makes 4 burgers.

Inside-out cheeseburgers

1 lb. ground beef
½ t. salt
dash pepper
processed American
   cheese, shredded
onions, chopped
dash barbecue sauce

Mix beef, salt, and pepper. Roll out patties (¼-in. thick) between sheets of wax paper. Top half the patties with a small amount of shredded cheese, chopped onions, and a dash of barbecue sauce, then cover with meat lids, pressing edges to seal. Broil over hot coals for 12–15 min., turning once.

Makes 3 burgers.

Barbecued burgers

1 lb. ground beef
¼ c. onions, chopped
2 T. green peppers,
  finely chopped,
  optional
3 T. ketchup
1 T. prepared
  horseradish
1 t. salt
2 t. prepared mustard
dash pepper

Mix all ingredients lightly. Shape into 4 patties about ½-in. thick. Broil over hot coals for 5 min., turn, and broil for 3 min. or to desired doneness.

Makes 4 burgers.

Taco burgers

1 lb. ground beef
1 can (16 oz.) tomatoes
1 pkg. taco seasoning
  mix
6 hamburger buns, split
  and toasted
1 c. Cheddar cheese (4
  oz.), shredded
2 c. lettuce, shredded

Brown beef until crumbly; drain off fat. Add tomatoes and seasoning mix. Stir well, breaking up large pieces of tomato. Bring to a boil. Reduce heat and simmer for 10 min. Spoon over toasted buns. Sprinkle with cheese and lettuce.

Makes 6 servings.

Burger toppings

Tangy topping

¼ c. mayonnaise
1 T. scallions, coarsely
    chopped
2 t. tarragon vinegar
dash dry mustard

Blend all ingredients.

Bacon blitz

¼ mayonnaise
grated horseradish to
    taste
crisp bacon, crumbled

Blend all ingredients.

Blue burger

¼ c. mayonnaise
¼ c. sour cream
¼ c. blue cheese,
    crumbled

Blend all ingredients.

Each recipe will top 3 large or 4 smaller burgers.

Franks

Franks

Franks, hot dogs, wieners—call them what you will—this popular relative of the sausage can be transformed into a mouth-watering array of sandwiches.

Ham-stuffed hot dogs

1 c. cooked ham or
   luncheon meat, finely
   chopped
3 T. pickle relish
2 T. onions, finely
   chopped
2 T. prepared mustard
2 T. mayonnaise
8–10 frankfurters
   (1 lb.)
8–10 slices bacon
bottled barbecue sauce
8–10 buns, toasted

Mix first 5 ingredients. Slit franks, ¾ through and almost to ends. Stuff with ham mixture, wrap with bacon, and secure with wooden toothpicks. Broil over hot coals, brushing with barbecue sauce, until filling is hot and bacon crisp. Serve in toasted buns.

Makes 8–10 servings.

Grilled cheese dogs

8 frankfurters
4 hamburger buns
butter
½ c. pickle relish
8 (1 oz.) slices Swiss
   cheese

On a broiler pan, broil frankfurters several inches from source of heat, turning frequently. Cut hamburger buns in half and butter cut side lightly. Toast buns until golden. Split frankfurters lengthwise, then cut each piece in half crosswise. Place 4 small pieces on bun half. Spread 1 tablespoon pickle relish over top and cover with 1 slice cheese. Broil until cheese melts. Serve immediately.

If a closed sandwich is desired, use 8 hamburger buns and top with other half of bun.

Makes 8 sandwiches.

Chili dogs

1 lb. ground beef
½ c. onions, chopped
1 can (15 oz.) chili with beans
5 frankfurters, cut diagonally in ¼ to ½-in. slices
1 can condensed tomato soup
½ c. chili sauce
¼ c. green peppers, chopped
8 hamburger buns, split and toasted

In a large skillet, lightly brown beef and onions; pour off fat. Add chili, frankfurters, soup, chili sauce, and green peppers and heat through. Serve over toasted buns.

Makes 8 servings.

Franks with sauerkraut and fruit

1 pkg. (11 oz.) mixed dried fruits, cut up
¾ c. onions, chopped
2 c. apple juice
3 T. brown sugar
1 can (16 oz.) sauerkraut, drained and rinsed
2 T. butter or margarine
1 t. caraway seed
½ t. salt
⅛ t. pepper
8–10 frankfurters (1 lb.), slashed at 1-in. intervals
4 t. cornstarch
2 T. water

Combine dried fruits, onions, apple juice, and sugar in a large saucepan or Dutch oven. Cover and cook for 10 min. Stir in remaining ingredients except cornstarch. Continue to cook over low heat for 10 min. Remove franks to serving dish. Blend cornstarch and water and add to sauerkraut mixture. Cook and stir until thickened. Combine with franks.

Makes 5–6 servings.

Franks

Hawaiian franks

3 T. brown sugar
1 T. cornstarch
¼ c. vinegar
¼ c. butter or
  margarine
8–10 frankfurter buns,
  toasted
8–10 frankfurters
  (1 lb.)
1 can (15 oz.) pineapple
  spears, drained,
  reserving ½ c. syrup
5 (1 oz.) slices boiled
  ham

In a skillet, cook sugar, cornstarch, reserved pineapple syrup, vinegar, and butter over medium heat until thick and bubbly. Brush inside of each bun with sauce. Slit franks lengthwise and place 1½ pineapple spears in each slit. Cut each ham slice into 4 strips. Wrap 2 ham strips around each frank; secure with wooden toothpicks. Grill over medium coals for 6 min., or until franks are done, basting occasionally with sauce. Serve in buns. Serve remaining sauce separately.

Makes 8–10 servings.

Fancy franks

1 c. apricot preserves
4 oz. tomato sauce
  (½ c.)
⅓ c. vinegar
¼ c. dry white wine
2 T. soy sauce
2 T. honey
1 T. salad oil
1 t. salt
¼ t. ground ginger
16–20 frankfurters
  (2 lb.)
8–10 buns, toasted

Mix first 9 ingredients. Score franks on the bias and broil over hot coals, turning and basting often with sauce. Serve on toasted buns. Heat remaining sauce to pass.

Makes 8–10 servings.

Shish-ka-bob

1 egg, slightly beaten
¾ c. soft bread crumbs
¼ c. milk
2 T. onions, chopped
½ t. salt
pinch pepper
1 lb. ground beef
6 frankfurters
1 c. ketchup
4 T. butter or
   margarine, melted
¼ c. molasses
2 T. vinegar
6 buns, toasted

Mix first 6 ingredients. Add beef and mix well. Divide into 6 portions and shape around franks, covering completely. Chill. Insert skewers through franks lengthwise. Broil 3-in. from heat for 15 min., turning often. Combine remaining ingredients, heat through, and brush on meat during the last 5 min. of cooking. Serve in toasted frankfurter buns.

Makes 6 servings.

Wieners wrapped and stuffed

Slit frankfurters lengthwise, but not quite through. Spread cut surfaces with prepared mustard and stuff with cheese strips, pineapple chunks, baked beans, drained sauerkraut, pickle relish, or mashed potatoes. Wrap each frank with bacon; secure ends with wooden toothpicks. Broil, stuffed-side down, on broiler rack set 3—4-in. from heat for 5 min. Turn and broil for 3—5 min. longer. Remove toothpicks and serve in toasted buns.

Pizza

Pizza

Are you wondering how pizza got into a sandwich cookbook? If you stop to think about it, pizza is really just a big open-face sandwich. When does pizza cease being a pizza and become just a big open-face sandwich? There are probably as many answers to this question as there are pizza parlors in the world. This chapter does not offer the definitive answer, but you will find some tasty pizza recipes to please diverse palates.

Pizza

1 pkg. active dry yeast
2 T. warm water
1 c. boiling water
2 T. shortening
½ t. salt
½ t. sugar
3 c. flour, sifted
olive oil
3 c. tomato sauce
½ lb. mozzarella cheese
oregano
Parmesan cheese

Preheat oven to 450° F.
Grease two 12-in.
  pizza pans with
  olive oil.

Soften yeast in warm water. Mix boiling water, shortening, salt, and sugar; cool to lukewarm and add to yeast. Add most of the flour and beat until smooth; add remaining flour and knead. Set in a greased bowl, covered, in a warm place until dough doubles in size. Punch down dough, divide in half. Place each half in pizza pan and press dough firmly into pan so that it comes well up on the sides. Brush with olive oil. Spread with tomato sauce and cover with thin slices of mozzarella. Sprinkle generously with oregano and grated Parmesan. Bake for ½ hour, until the crust is blistered and well browned and the cheese melts.

Variations. Any of the following ingredients may be added to the filling: cooked, sliced Italian sausages; lightly sautéed mushrooms; or anchovies. Provolone or other good melting cheeses may be used instead of mozzarella.

Makes 2 pizzas.

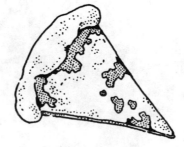

THE SANDWICH COOKBOOK

Sicilian tomato pizza pie

1 pkg. active dry yeast
1 t. lukewarm water
1 lb. flour
1 t. salt
8 anchovy fillets
2 T. peanut or olive oil
2 c. plain tomato sauce
½ c. Pecorino cheese,
  grated

Preheat oven to 450° F.
Grease a large baking
  pan

Dissolve yeast in lukewarm water. Place sifted flour and salt on a board and add dissolved yeast. Knead thoroughly for 15 min., add oil, and continue kneading until smooth ball is formed. Cover well and set aside in a warm place for 3 hours or until dough has doubled in size. Cut anchovies into small pieces; add to the tomato sauce. When dough has risen, spread in a large greased baking pan; dough should be ½ to ¾-in. thick. Dent here and there with fingers. Pour generous layer of sauce over dough and sprinkle with grated cheese. Bake for ½ hour. Lower heat and continue baking for 15 min., or until pizza is golden. Remove from oven. Cut into 4 to 5-in. squares. Serve very hot.

Makes 4–6 servings.

Pizza with sausage

Follow same recipe and quantities as for Sicilian tomato pizza pie. Cut ½ pound of Italian sausage into small pieces and arrange on dough before adding the sauce and cheese. Bake as for Sicilian tomato pizza pie.

Cheddar-mozzarella mini-pizzas

4 large English muffins,
  split and buttered
Parmesan cheese
1 c. Cheddar cheese,
  shredded (4 oz.)
4 frankfurters
1 can (8 oz.) pizza
  sauce
½ c. mozzarella cheese,
  shredded (2 oz.)

Sprinkle muffin halves with Parmesan cheese and toast under broiler until golden. Place 2 tablespoons Cheddar cheese on each muffin half. Cut frankfurters crosswise into ¼-in. slices; arrange on muffins. Top each with 2 tablespoons pizza sauce and sprinkle with 1 tablespoon mozzarella. Bake in oven for 12–15 min., or until thoroughly heated.

Makes 4 servings.

Preheat oven to 350° F.

Pizza snacks

½ lb. Italian sausage
1 t. dried oregano,
  crushed
1 clove garlic, minced
1 pkg. (8 oz.)
  refrigerated biscuits
  (10 biscuits)
tomato paste
4 oz. sharp processed
  American cheese,
  shredded (1 c.)
¼ c. Parmesan cheese,
  grated

Brown sausage; drain. Add oregano and garlic. On a greased baking sheet, flatten biscuits to 4-in. circles with a floured custard cup; leave rim. Fill with tomato paste and sausage. Sprinkle with cheeses. Bake for 10 min.

Makes 3–5 servings.

Preheat oven to 425° F.

Super sandwiches

Super sandwiches

These are sandwiches for big appetites and for appetites seeking a change from the usual.

Longboy hero sandwich

1 long, thick loaf French or Italian bread
1 clove garlic, cut
butter or margarine, softened
½ lb. bologna, sliced
½ lb. Italian salami, sliced
½ lb. cooked smoked tongue, sliced
½ lb. cooked ham, thinly sliced
chicory
2 large firm ripe tomatoes, thickly sliced
1 large Spanish onion, thinly sliced
12 slices Muenster cheese
6 strips bacon, crisply cooked
green olives

Slice off top horizontal third of loaf. Rub cut sides of both pieces with garlic and spread with softened butter. On bottom piece, arrange layers of meat, vegetables, and cheese. Garnish with bacon and olives. Replace top of loaf. Slice in serving pieces. Serve with pickle relish, mustard, dill pickles, pickled red peppers, French dressing, and potato salad.

Makes 6–8 servings.

Ham, egg, and cheese

½ c. mayonnaise
4 hard-boiled eggs, chopped
2 T. sweet pickle relish
salt and pepper to taste
1 loaf French or Italian bread, cut in half
8 slices American cheese
10 slices boiled ham, cut in half lengthwise

Mix first 5 ingredients. Cover bread with cheese. Put 1 tablespoon egg mixture on end of each ham slice and roll up. Place ham rolls side by side on cheese. Broil 5-in. from heat source for 3–4 min., or until cheese melts.

Makes 6–8 servings.

Big hero sandwich

4 short loaves Italian
  bread or crusty rolls
¼ c. olive oil
¼ c. vinegar
½ t. oregano
½ lb. each salami,
  bologna, or other cold
  cuts
½ lb. Italian cheese
  (provolone or your
  choice), sliced
Italian peppers
  (optional)

Slice bread in half horizontally. Mix oil, vinegar, and oregano and lightly sprinkle on each bread slice. Layer slices of meat and cheese on lower half of bread. Add drained Italian peppers. Replace top of loaf. Shredded lettuce, chopped onions, and thinly sliced tomato may be added. Do not make sandwich in advance, since it becomes soggy.

Makes 4 servings.

Italian sandwich boat

1 loaf Italian or French
  bread
½ c. milk
1 egg
salt, pepper, and garlic
  to taste
1½ c. meat, fish, or
  poultry, diced
1½ c. celery, diced
⅓ c. olives, green or
  ripe, diced
½ c. mayonnaise
2 hard-boiled eggs,
  sliced
butter, melted

Cut off top crust of bread and reserve. Scoop out soft crumbs from bottom. Slice boat into desired number of servings, but do not cut bottom crust. Soak the removed bread crumbs in milk and blend in raw egg and seasonings. Add meat or poultry, celery, olives, and mayonnaise; mix well. Fill cavity of boat; top with egg slices. Replace crust cover. Brush outside of loaf with melted butter. Wrap in aluminum foil and bake for 30–40 min. Serve hot.

Makes 4–6 servings.

Preheat oven to 425° F.

Submarine sandwiches

Brown giant brown-and-serve French rolls (about 8-in. long) according to package directions. Split rolls lengthwise, but not quite through. Scoop out centers and spread loaves generously with prepared mustard, garlic butter, and/or mayonnaise with curry powder. Line bottoms of rolls with leaf lettuce. Pile on slices of corned beef, boiled ham, bologna, salami, pickled tongue, chicken, tuna, and herring as desired. Add slices of American and Swiss cheese, onions, green and ripe olives, and dill pickles. Secure sandwich with toothpicks.

Makes 1 large serving.

Sliced chicken, ham, and cheese hero

French or Italian bread
butter
5 slices chicken
3 slices ham
2 slices Swiss cheese

Cut loaf into 6-in. sections. Cut the sections in half and butter them. Place 5 thin slices of chicken meat on bottom half of bread. Put 3 slices of ham on the other half of bread. Put both halves under the broiler, about 6-in. from heat, for about 1 min.; don't brown the meat. Remove from oven and cover meat with cheese. Return to broiler until cheese melts. Put halves together and toast the top crust under broiler for 15 seconds.

Makes 3–4 sandwiches.

Meatball heroes

6 (8-in.) loaves Italian
    bread
3 T. butter, melted
¾ c. brown gravy,
    homemade or canned
¾ c. canned tomato
    sauce
½ T. prepared mustard
¾ c. Parmesan cheese,
    grated
½ lb. mozzarella cheese,
    sliced
¾ c. fresh parsley,
    minced

Slice off tops of bread loaves and hollow out loaf interiors. Brush interiors with melted butter. Mix gravy, tomato sauce, and mustard. Heat mixture and spread in the bottom of each loaf. Cover with meatballs (see below) in 1 layer. Dust with Parmesan cheese and top with mozzarella cheese and parsley. Bake for 20 min. in 350° F. oven, or until sizzling hot.

Italian meatballs
½ c. white bread, finely
    crumbled
1 c. water
2 t. beef broth powder
1 lb. twice-ground beef,
    or equal parts beef,
    pork, and veal
½ c. Parmesan cheese,
    grated
2 t. salt
½ t. pepper
½ t. ground basil
¼ t. garlic powder
2 T. tart apple, peeled
    and grated
½ c. onions, peeled and
    finely chopped
3 T. flour
¼ c. olive oil

Mix all meatball ingredients except flour and oil. Shape into small marble-sized balls. Dust with flour and let stand for 10 min. Brown all over in hot oil, then slowly sauté for 4 min.

Makes 6 sandwiches.

Preheat oven to 350° F.

Sausage and peppers hero

1 ripe tomato
2 links Italian sausage
½ green pepper
salt and pepper to taste
1 T. olive oil
½ c. tomato sauce
Italian bread

Make tomato sauce by slicing tomato, putting slices in a cup, and mashing with a fork. Slice the sausage and green pepper in ¼-in. pieces. Sauté sausage in hot oil in a frying pan over medium heat; cook for 1 min., stirring now and then. Add the green peppers and sprinkle with salt and pepper. Stir the meat and peppers for 2 min. Stir in tomato sauce. Spread mixture over bottom of pan, cover, and simmer for 3—4 min. Cut the bread in 6-in. sections and slice them in half. Spoon sausage and peppers onto bottom halves of bread.

Makes 4—6 servings.

Tuna fish boats

1 can (6½ or 7 oz.)
    tuna fish, drained
½ c. celery, chopped
¼ c. mayonnaise, or
    bottled lemon juice
    and softened butter
soft long rolls
parsley, if desired

Mix tuna, celery, and mayonnaise. Hollow out rolls, leaving ½-in. shell. Fill with tuna mixture. Decorate with sprigs of parsley.

Makes 4—5 sandwiches.

Club sandwich

3 slices sandwich bread,
    toasted
butter or margarine
lettuce
cooked chicken or
    turkey, sliced
mayonnaise or salad
    dressing
2–3 thin slices tomato
2–3 slices cooked
    bacon

Spread butter on toast. Top a slice with lettuce and chicken; spread with mayonnaise. Top with second slice and add tomato and bacon. Top with third slice and anchor with 4 toothpicks. Cut diagonally in quarters.

Makes 1 sandwich.

Triple decker club

1–2 T. coleslaw
mayonnaise
salt and pepper to taste
3 slices toast
1 thin slice boiled ham
1 slice cooked turkey or
    chicken breast
1 large or 2 small slices
    tomato, peeled

Make coleslaw by shredding cabbage in a bowl and adding a little salt and pepper and enough mayonnaise to make it moist. Bring the ham, turkey and slaw to room temperature. Butter 2 slices toast; spread mayonnaise thinly on the third slice. Lay turkey on the mayonnaise-covered slice. Add tomato and salt. Cover the turkey with the dry side of 1 slice of buttered toast. Add ham and top with coleslaw. Cover with the third slice of buttered toast, buttered-side down.

Makes 1 sandwich.

Ham and cheese pita pocket

1 can (3 oz.) deviled
    ham or deviled
    chicken
2 T. mayonnaise
2 T. celery, chopped
¼ c. cheese, shredded
2 small pita bread
    pockets

Mix ham, mayonnaise, celery, and cheese. Spoon into pita.

Makes 2 sandwiches.

Super sandwiches

Sardine or tuna pita pocket

2 sardines, chopped, or
  tuna, flaked
2 T. sweet pickle relish
2 T. mayonnaise
¼ c. cheese, shredded
2 small pita bread
  pockets

Mix sardines or tuna, relish, mayonnaise, and cheese.
Spoon mixture into pita.

Makes 2 sandwiches.

Vegetable pita pocket

¼ c. bean sprouts
¼ c. combination of
  chopped celery,
  carrots, green
  peppers, and
  mushrooms
1–2 T. ranch-style or
  Thousand Island
  dressing
pita bread

Mix bean sprouts and vegetables. Add dressing to
moisten. Stuff into small pita pocket.

Makes 1–2 servings.

Easy popovers

1 c. flour
½ t. salt
1 c. milk
2 eggs

Beat ingredients with rotary beater until smooth. Pour
into buttered muffin tins (¾ full) or large custard
cups (½ full). Bake at 425° F. for 40–45 min., until
golden brown. Serve immediately with desired filling.

Makes 6 popovers.

Ricotta cheese and peanut butter

½ c. peanut butter
¼ c. cheese, grated
¼ c. ricotta cheese
1 T. honey
1 t. cinnamon

Mix ingredients well until blended.

Makes enough filling for 2—4 popovers.

Scrapple popover

¼ c. apple butter
¼ c. Cheddar cheese,
  shredded

Mix ingredients well until blended.

Makes enough spread for 2—4 popovers.

Super sandwiches

Keep-trim
sandwiches

Keep-trim sandwiches

Sandwiches do not have to be loaded with calories to be tasty and appealing. When made with "keep-trim" fillings and thinly sliced breads, they can be delicious and satisfying yet lower in calories. Spread the bread with a thin layer of filling and leave out all butter or margarine, mayonnaise, or salad dressing. Lettuce can be used to make a fuller sandwich without adding calories. (If the sandwich has to be carried, pack the lettuce separately and tuck it into the sandwich at mealtime.)

Use seasonings generously—a thin but tasty sandwich is more satisfying than a thick, tasteless one. If the sandwich is part of lunch, fresh fruit, vegetable nibblers, and a beverage will round out the meal well.

Double cheese sandwich

Combine Roquefort and Neufchatel* cheeses. Add a bit of minced onion or a dash of onion juice and some well-drained, chopped canned mushrooms. Spread on dark bread.
*Neufchatel cheese has 32 percent fewer calories than cream cheese.

Bacon and cottage cheese sandwich

Combine crumbled cooked bacon or bacon-flavored vegetable-protein bits with chopped sweet gherkins. Moisten with blended cottage cheese. (Cottage cheese, blended smooth in blender with a bit of water or milk, makes a tasty, lower-calorie alternate for sour cream.) Spread on toast.

Chicken and olive sandwich

Mix chopped cooked chicken with chopped ripe olives. Add just enough low-calorie mayonnaise to moisten. Spread on raisin bread.

Crunchy tuna sandwich

Mix tuna, minced celery, chopped nuts, salt, and a bit of blended cottage cheese. Spread on thin slices of date-nut bread.

Apple-and-ham sandwich

Spread apple butter on rye or pumpernickel bread. Add a couple slices boiled ham.

Hawaiian sandwich

Mix cottage cheese, drained canned crushed pineapple, and a bit of onion salt. Spread on raisin bread.

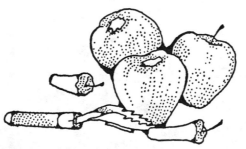

Keep-trim sandwiches

Chicken liver special sandwich

Chop cooked chicken livers with stuffed olives. Spread on pumpernickel bread.

Deli sandwich

Place a slice of baked ham or roast beef between 2 slices of rye or pumpernickel. Add coleslaw made with low-calorie mayonnaise.

Peppery sandwich

Sandwich thinly sliced green pepper and ham or beef slices between slices of dark or white bread.

Chili-meat sandwich

Chop canned luncheon meat and moisten it with chili sauce. Spread on rye bread.

Curried shrimp sandwich

Mix canned shrimp and chopped apples with low-calorie mayonnaise and curry powder. Spread on dark bread.

Cheese-and-orange sandwich

Spread Neufchatel cheese and orange marmalade on raisin bread or toast.

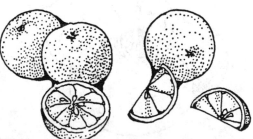

Cottage cheese sandwich spread

Because cottage cheese is so bland, it can be used with strong seasonings as a snappy spread for sandwiches. Serve with a vegetable garnish and top off with fresh or stewed fruit and coffee or tea for a refreshing luncheon.

Cottage cheese anchovy filling

Finely chop 6 anchovies and mix with 8 ounces creamed or skim-milk cottage cheese. Stir in 2 tablespoons each of minced radishes and pickle relish.

Cottage cheese tomato filling

Finely chop 1 large peeled tomato. Add 1 tablespoon minced chives, ½ teaspoon mustard, ½ teaspoon crushed caraway seeds, and 8 ounces creamed or skim-milk cottage cheese, and stir until puréed.

THE SANDWICH COOKBOOK

Hungarian cottage cheese spread

Great on rye or pumpernickel bread. It is usually served plain, but shrimp or chopped raw vegetables may be added to it.

½ lb. cottage cheese
3 T. butter, softened
½ t. salt
black pepper to taste
1 t. paprika
1 t. Dijon mustard
2 T. onions, finely
    chopped
2 anchovies, finely
    chopped
2 t. capers
1 t. caraway seeds,
    optional
½ c. plain yogurt

Combine all ingredients except yogurt; beat until creamy. Chill for 2 hours. Stir in the yogurt. Spread on 1 slice of bread and serve as an open-face sandwich.

Makes 4 servings.

Ham and salad rolls

4 frankfurter buns, split
4 t. prepared mustard
1 c. lettuce, shredded
¼ c. cucumber, chopped
2 T. low-calorie French-
    style salad dressing
8 thin slices boiled ham
4 dill pickle strips

Spread mustard on cut sides of buns. Mix lettuce, cucumber, and dressing. Place ¼ of mixture at end of a stack of 2 ham slices; top with 1 pickle. Roll up and secure with toothpicks. Place in bun.

Makes 4 servings.

Cottage cheese sandwiches

1½ c. small curd cream-
   style cottage cheese
½ c. celery, diced
¼ c. carrots, shredded
¼ c. radish, chopped
½ t. caraway seeds
6 slices thinly sliced
   white bread
1 T. butter, softened
6 lettuce leaves

Mash cheese with fork, then stir in celery, carrots, radish, and caraway seeds. Chill. Spread butter on bread. Top with lettuce. Spread each sandwich with ⅓ cup of cheese mixture.

Makes 6 servings.

Open-face chicken sandwiches

2 T. all-purpose flour
1 T. sugar
1 t. dry mustard
½ t. salt
dash of cayenne pepper
2 egg yolks, slightly
   beaten
¾ c. skim milk
3 T. vinegar
1 can (5 oz.) water
   chestnuts
paprika
8 slices whole wheat
   bread
watercress
8 slices cooked chicken

Blend flour, sugar, mustard, salt, and cayenne. Stir in yolks and milk. Simmer over low heat, stirring until thick and bubbly. Stir in vinegar. Chill. Drain and slice water chestnuts. Roll edges of a few water chestnuts in paprika; set aside. Spread bread with dressing; top with 5 sprigs watercress, 1 slice of chicken, and a few water chestnuts. Top finally with a few slices of paprika-edged water chestnuts. Serve remaining dressing separately.

Makes 8 servings.

Broiled ham-asparagus-cheese sandwiches

1 pkg. (10 oz.) frozen
   asparagus spears
4 slices white bread,
   toasted
2 t. prepared mustard
4 slices boiled ham
2 oz. processed Swiss
   cheese, shredded
   (½ c.)
2 T. green onions,
   chopped
1 T. canned pimento,
   chopped

Cook asparagus according to package directions; drain well and keep warm. Spread mustard on 1 side of each slice of toast. Place ham slices on bread and hot asparagus spears atop ham. Mix cheese, green onions, and chopped pimento; sprinkle over asparagus. Broil 5-in. from heat for 2—3 min., until cheese melts.

Makes 4 sandwiches.

Cream cheese and fresh fruit bagels

2 bagels, split and
   toasted
1 T. cream cheese,
   softened
ground cinnamon
1 med. peach
½ med. banana
ascorbic acid or lemon
   juice
4 thin slices honeydew
   melon

Spread cream cheese on toasted bagels; sprinkle with cinnamon. Dip peach and banana slices in ascorbic acid or lemon juice to prevent darkening. Place sliced fruit and honeydew atop bagels.

Makes 4 servings.

Cucumber sandwiches

Mix vinegar, water, sugar, salt, dill, and pepper; add cucumber. Cover and chill for 3 hours; stir occasionally. Drain. Spread butter on bread and top with cucumber and thinly sliced radishes.

~~water~~
1 t. sugar
¼ t. salt
¼ t. dried dill weed
dash of pepper
1 large unpeeled
   cucumber, thinly
   sliced
4 slices white bread
4 t. butter
4 radishes, thinly sliced

Makes 4 servings.

Hot cheese and egg sandwich

4 hard-boiled eggs,
   chopped
½ c. low-calorie
   mayonnaise-type
   dressing
2 T. sweet pickle relish
2 T. green onions,
   chopped
1 T. prepared mustard
6 slices white bread,
   toasted
3 slices mozzarella
   cheese (4½ oz.),
   halved
6 thin slices tomato
salt to taste

Mix eggs, dressing, relish, green onions, and mustard, then spread on bread. Broil 4-in. from heat for 3–4 min., until heated through. Top each sandwich with a cheese slice and tomato slice. Sprinkle with salt. Broil until cheese melts.

Makes 6 sandwiches.

Open-face salmon sandwich

1 can (7¾ oz.) pink
  salmon, drained,
  flaked, and bones
  removed
⅓ c. low-calorie
  mayonnaise-type
  dressing
1 can (5 oz.) water
  chestnuts, drained
  and finely chopped
1 T. green onions, sliced
1 t. soy sauce
1 t. lemon juice
6 slices rye bread
6 cherry tomatoes

Mix salmon, dressing, water chestnuts, onions, soy
sauce, and lemon juice thoroughly. Spread mixture on
bread slices. Top each sandwich with a tomato.

Makes 6 servings.

Tuna salad sandwich

1 can (6½ oz.) water-
  pack tuna, drained
⅓ c. cream-style cottage
  cheese
⅓ c. celery, chopped
1 T. sweet pickle,
  chopped
1 T. onions, chopped
1 T. low-calorie
  mayonnaise-type
  dressing
¼ t. salt
4 slices rye bread
lettuce
4 slices tomato

Blend first 7 ingredients. Spread dressing on rye bread
and top with a lettuce leaf and tomato slice. Season
with salt. Spoon tuna mixture atop tomatoes.

Makes 4 servings.

Fancy broiled crab sandwiches

1 can (7½ oz.) crab
   meat, drained, flaked,
   and cartilage removed
¼ c. low-calorie
   mayonnaise-type
   dressing
1 oz. processed
   American cheese
   (¼ c.), shredded
¼ c. celery, finely
   chopped
1 T. canned pimento,
   chopped
2 t. lemon juice
3 English muffins, split
   and toasted
parsley, optional

Mix first 5 ingredients. Spread about ¼ cup of mixture atop each muffin half. Broil 5-in. from heat for 2–3 min., until cheese melts. Garnish with parsley, if desired.

Makes 6 servings.

Stacked-up shrimp sandwiches

2 (4½ oz.) cans shrimp,
  drained, deveined,
  and chopped
1 T. lemon juice
¼ c. celery, diced
2 T. sweet pickle,
  chopped
2 T. green onions, thinly
  sliced
¼ t. salt
dash of pepper
⅓ c. low-calorie
  mayonnaise-type
  dressing
3 English muffins, split
  and toasted
6 leaves Boston lettuce
6 tomato slices
1 hard-boiled egg, sliced

Sprinkle lemon juice on shrimp. Gently mix in celery, sweet pickle, green onions, salt, pepper, and dressing. Chill. Top each muffin half with a lettuce leaf and tomato slice. Spoon about ⅓ cup of shrimp mixture atop each tomato slice. Top with egg slices.

Makes 6 servings.

Sandwiches for parties

Sandwiches for parties

Sandwiches are ideal for parties. They can be made in advance. They are easy to serve and easy to eat. And they can be pretty to look at as well as pleasing to the palate. (You don't really need to wait for your next party to try the recipes in this chapter.)

Fancy shapes for sandwiches

One of the best ways to achieve diversity in the meals we serve is through visual appeal. In addition to the use of color and texture, various shapes can be employed to make sandwiches more interesting.

Bread and butter sandwiches

Spread softened butter on slices of brown and white bread. Top brown slices with white bread and white slices with brown bread. Cut sandwiches into quarters. Place on platter alternating dark with light.

Ribbon sandwiches

Put a slice of white bread on a slice of dark bread, spreading filling between slices; repeat. Press together, wrap, and chill. Trim crusts, if necessary, and cut in ½-in. slices.

Mosaic sandwiches

Remove crusts from one unsliced loaf each of white and dark bread; cut soft inner part into thin slices lengthwise. Spread half the slices with creamed butter and any sandwich filling. Cut out small shapes from remaining slices. Place dark cutouts in the spaces of white bread, and white designs in the spaces of dark bread. Cover each slice spread with filling with a 2-color slice. Cut into desired shapes.

Checkerboard sandwiches

Remove top crust from unsliced loaves of white and whole wheat bread. Cut 3 slices (½-in.) lengthwise from each loaf. Spread slices with creamed butter and any sandwich filling. Put together alternate slices of dark and white bread. Press slices together, put in refrigerator, and place plate on top of pile. When filling is firm, cut off crusts. Cut each pile crosswise into ½-in. slices. Spread cut sides with creamed butter and sandwich filling; put together, alternating brown and white slices. Place in refrigerator again, under a light weight, until butter is firm. Then cut crosswise into thin slices. Arrange on platter to show checkerboard pattern.

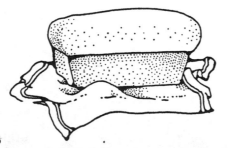

Pinwheel sandwiches

Cut crusts from unsliced fresh bread. Slice lengthwise as thinly as possible. Flatten slightly with rolling pin. Spread evenly with creamed butter and any sandwich filling. Roll each slice tightly and then wrap in foil or plastic. Refrigerate seam-side down, until firm. To serve, cut in thin slices crosswise.

Watercress pinwheels

1 loaf unsliced white
   sandwich bread
1 c. watercress, snipped
2 (3 oz.) pkg. cream
   cheese, softened
dash of salt

Slice bread lengthwise in ⅜-in. slices. Remove crusts. Mix watercress, cheese, and salt. Spread ¼ cup of filling on each slice. Roll up from narrow end. Wrap in foil and chill. Slice pinwheels ¾-in thick.

Makes 21 pinwheels.

Tomato ring sandwiches

Cut circular slices of bread and remove insides of half of these to form rings. Spread large rounds with softened butter, then cover with lettuce and mayonnaise. Place a ring over lettuce and fill center with tomato slice or tomato aspic cut into rounds. Use any desired combination of fillings. The cutout rounds may also be spread and served separately.

Rolled picnic sandwiches

Cut off crusts from a loaf of unsliced white bread. Thinly slice the loaf and spread with softened butter or cream cheese. Top with chopped watercress leaves or thin slices of scallions. Roll up like a jelly roll. Garnish each end with a sprig of watercress. Wrap tightly in aluminum foil or Saran wrap. Chill until ready to serve.

Variation. Roquefort or Danish blue cheese mixed with a little softened butter or with petit Suisse cheese makes a flavorful spread for these sandwiches.

Jigsaw sandwiches

1 pkg. (3 oz.) cream cheese, softened
1 T. milk
1 t. Worcestershire sauce
4–5 slices bacon, crisply cooked and crumbled
white, whole wheat, and rye bread slices

Mix cream cheese, milk, Worcestershire sauce, and bacon. Cut bread slices into 2-in. rounds. For smooth edges, freeze breads and cut while frozen. Spread half the assorted rounds with cheese mixture. Top with remaining rounds made into double rounds or stripes. For double rounds, cut shapes from centers of rounds and fit together contrasting breads. For stripes, cut rounds into 3 strips so that center strip is widest; fit large strip between 2 smaller strips of contrasting bread and hold them together with bits of cheese.

Teatime sandwiches

2 (3 oz.) pkg. cream cheese, softened
⅓ c. mayonnaise
2 T. blue cheese, crumbled
½ c. nuts, finely chopped
¼ t. salt
¼ t. onions, grated
½ t. Worcestershire sauce
bread rounds, lightly buttered

Mix first 7 ingredients. Chill. Spread on bread.

Makes 1⅓ cups spread.

Egg and watercress sandwiches

Chop hard-boiled eggs and mix with melted butter to form a paste. Season to taste with mustard, salt, white pepper, grated onions, and vinegar. Spread on bread slices, arrange watercress over mixture, and top with bread. Trim crusts. Cut into strips or triangles.

Cucumber sandwiches

Thinly slice a cucumber. Soak slices in vinegar for a few min. Drain. Season with salt and black pepper. Place between thin slices of buttered bread. Trim crusts. Cut into strips or triangles.

Toast baskets

Make 2 cuts (2-in. deep and 1¼-in. apart) in top center of small round loaf of bread; cut down to within 1½-in. of bottom. Cut off sides to within 1½-in. of bottom, and leave top strip intact at end for handle. Scoop out bread to form a basket. Toast basket lightly under broiler. Fill with scrambled eggs and bacon or sausage.

Toast chests

Cut 1-in. slice from top of small loaf of unsliced bread and set aside. Scoop out inside of bottom part of loaf. Toast under broiler. Fill with scrambled eggs, creamed chicken, or chipped beef. Replace top. Serve at once.

Toast cups and cornucopias

For toast cups, trim slices of white or other bread and shape into muffin tins. Toast under broiler. Fill with eggs or creamed dishes. For cornucopias, trim slices of fresh bread and roll up starting at one corner of square. Pin each with a toothpick to form a cornucopia. Toast lightly under broiler. Line with baked ham and fill with scrambled or creamed eggs.

Toast points

Trim bread and cut into triangles. Butter and place in basket or bowl with large angle up. Or, serve around eggs or a meat dish.

Sandwiches for parties

Toast rounds, rings, or knots

Trim and cut bread into rounds. For rings, cut a hole in the center of each round. For knots, cut out narrow rectangles and tie into loose knots. For a variation on rings, pull 2 narrow rectangles through the center of each ring.

Toast sticks, logs, or fingers

Trim and cut bread into rectangles. Toast. Butter pieces and dip into seeds, toasted coconut, or cheese.

Cinnamon toast

4 slices bread
2 T. sugar
1 t. cinnamon
1 t. butter, melted

Mix sugar, cinnamon, and butter. Toast bread on 1 side. Spread mixture on untoasted side. Place under broiler until mixture bubbles.

Honey toast

6 slices whole-wheat
  bread
2 T. honey
2 T. butter
⅛ t. ground cardamom

Blend honey, butter, and cardamom until smooth. Toast bread on 1 side. Spread honey mixture on untoasted side. Place under broiler until brown.

Maple nut toast

¼ c. maple sugar,
  crushed
2 T. butter, melted
¼ c. pecans, chopped
6 slices sesame-egg
  bread, toasted

Combine sugar, butter, and nuts. Spread mixture on toast.

Melba toast

Lightly brown very thin slices of white bread in 200°−250° F. oven.

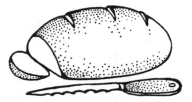

Orange toast

2 T. frozen orange juice
  concentrate
¼ c. sugar
2 t. butter, softened
¼ t. orange rind, grated
6 slices bread, toasted

Combine orange juice, sugar, butter, and orange rind. Spread on toast. Place briefly under broiler.

Seed toast

2 t. light corn syrup
2 T. butter
½ t. vanilla
2 T. poppy or sesame
  seeds
4 slices white bread,
  toasted

Mix syrup, butter, vanilla, and seeds. Spread seed mixture on toast. Place under broiler until seeds start to brown.

Coconut toast

3 T. butter, softened
¼ c. fine granulated
  sugar
¼ c. coconut, finely
  shredded
6 slices bread, toasted

Mix butter, sugar, and coconut. Spread mixture on toast. Place under broiler until brown.

Apple cheese toast

Spread apple butter on toast and sprinkle with shredded mild American cheese. Place under broiler until cheese melts.

Banana toast

6 slices bread, toasted
2 ripe bananas
1 T. lemon juice
3 T. sugar
2 T. butter, melted

Mash bananas and mix with lemon juice and butter. Spread on toast. Place under broiler until bananas brown slightly.

Butterscotch toast

2 T. brown sugar
4 slices bread, toasted
2 T. butter, softened

Mix butter and brown sugar. Spread on toast. Place under broiler until sugar bubbles.

Cheese toast

4 slices rye bread
1 T. butter
1 c. Gruyère cheese,
  shredded

Toast bread on 1 side. Butter untoasted side and spread with cheese. Place under broiler until cheese melts and browns slightly.

Canapés

Canapés are small, open sandwiches. This French word means "sofa." Thus, the sardine, cheese, or whatever kind of tidbit rests on a sofa, in this case a small piece of bread. Except for size, canapés and sandwiches are much alike.

Rainbow canapé wheel

Remove lower crust from a large, round rye bread loaf. Cut a thin round slice from the bottom and spread thickly with butter and mayonnaise. Place this slice on a platter and decorate with circles made of a variety of sandwich mixtures. Mark a circle in center with tumbler; spread caviar in this circle. For a second circle, use a 5-in. plate as a marker; spread hard-boiled yolks in this circle. For third ring, use minced ham; fourth, whites of hard-boiled eggs; fifth, stuffed olives; sixth, mixed yolks and whites of hard-boiled eggs. Remove crust. Cut in small wedges.

THE SANDWICH COOKBOOK

Harlequin canapés

Remove crusts from a square loaf of rye bread. Cut loaf lengthwise into ½-in. slices. Spread creamed butter and mayonnaise on each slice. Mark 8 parallel lines lengthwise on slice, through butter and mayonnaise, ½-in. apart. Spread sandwich fillings of contrasting colors between lines. In center, put finely ground smoked salmon. On both sides of salmon, put finely chopped, hard-boiled egg whites. In next spaces, riced yolks. Then sardine paste. Decorate space at either end with softened cream cheese pressed through a pastry tube. Slice crosswise into 1-in. strips and arrange on oblong platters.

Crab meat canapés

1 can crab meat, picked
   over
¼ c. mayonnaise
1 T. parsley, chopped
1 T. chives, chopped
1 t. lemon juice
1 t. Worcestershire sauce
Tabasco sauce to taste
black pepper to taste
toast rounds

Mix crab meat, mayonnaise, herbs, and seasonings. Spread on toast rounds. Serve immediately.

Makes 16 canapés.

Sardine canapés

1 can boneless sardines,
  drained
2 t. lemon juice
1 T. cream
½ t. dry mustard
1 T. mayonnaise
black pepper to taste
few drops of Tabasco
  sauce
toast rounds
hard-boiled egg slices or
  sliced green olives

Mash the sardines with a fork. Mix in mayonnaise and seasonings. Spread on toast rounds. Garnish with olives or egg slices.

Makes 12 small canapés.

Shrimp canapés

18 med. shrimp, cooked,
  shelled, deveined, and
  halved lengthwise
12 toast rounds, buttered
mayonnaise
12 sprigs fresh dill
lemon wedges
black pepper to taste

Place 3 shrimp halves in a spiral on each toast round. Garnish, if desired, with mayonnaise "stars" pressed from a pastry tube. Top with dill. Serve with lemon wedges and black pepper.

Makes 6 servings.

Smoked salmon canapés

Spread butter on toast. Place a thin round of smoked salmon on top. Border with hard-boiled eggs mixed with minced parsley.

Anchovy-butter canapés

Spread anchovy butter on triangle-shaped toast. Sprinkle chopped whites of hard-boiled eggs along 1 side. On second side, chopped yolks. On third side, minced pickles. Place a stuffed olive in center.

Caviar with eggs

Slice hard-boiled eggs; remove yolks and fill their spaces with caviar. Serve on thin buttered slices of brown bread. Arrange riced yolks as a border.

Sandwiches for parties

Caviar with onions

Blend 4 parts caviar with 1 part mayonnaise. Spread on buttered bread or toast. Sprinkle with grated or chopped onions.

Caviar with potato chips

Chill one 3-ounce can caviar. Season caviar with lemon juice. Spread on large potato chips. Garnish with border of cream cheese.

Chicken liver canapés

Sauté a dozen chicken livers in hot fat or butter with minced onion until tender. Mash to a paste. Add salt, cayenne, butter, and anchovy paste to taste. Spread on toast. Calves' liver may be used in place of chicken livers.

THE SANDWICH COOKBOOK

Chicken liver and mushroom canapés

Sauté chicken livers in hot fat or butter for a few min. Drain and mash. Sauté chopped mushrooms. Mix mushrooms and liver; add lemon juice, onion juice, salt, and pepper to taste. Spread on buttered toast.

Pickled herring canapés I

Bone and chop ½ pound pickled herring tidbits and cream with 4 tablespoons butter. Add parsley. Spread on fresh rye bread or toast. Separate hard-boiled eggs; finely chop the whites and rice the yolks. Decorate canapés with the egg.

Pickled herring canapés II

Bone and mash ½ pound pickled herring tidbits and add 2 tablespoons cream cheese, 2 tablespoons sweet butter, a little grated onion, and a pinch of cayenne pepper. Spread on toast rounds or triangles.

Tartare canapés

Season freshly ground raw beef with salt and onion juice. Spread beef on rye toast rounds. Or, omit onion juice and top with onion slice.

Avocado canapés

Cut off crusts from thin slices of white and dark bread. Spread with butter and seasoned mayonnaise. Place thin slices of cold roast turkey or chicken on white bread, add a layer of thinly sliced avocado, and top with a slice of dark bread. Wrap in a damp towel and refrigerate for a few hours. Cut into small wedges and set upright in pyramids on a tray ringed with parsley. Toothpicks may be used to hold the wedges together.

Anchovy and curry canapés

Finely chop the contents of 1 can flat anchovy fillets with ¼ cup softened sweet butter, 1 teaspoon crumbled blue cheese, and 1 teaspoon curry powder. Add 1–2 drops Worcestershire sauce, if desired, and spread on toast fingers.

Makes 8–12 canapés.

Cucumber canapés

Trim crusts from fresh bread slices; cut each slice into 4 equal squares. Spread with softened butter or mayonnaise. Peel cucumbers and cut into wafer-thin slices. Layer cucumber slices on bread squares. Serve with salt, lemon wedges, and black pepper.

Canapés Sagroniz

6 T. Roquefort cheese
1 T. butter
1 t. sour cream
3 slices white bread,
    toasted
6 T. caviar
lemon juice

Mix cheese, butter, and sour cream. Spread cheese mixture on toast and top each slice with 2 tablespoons caviar. Add a few drops of lemon juice. Cut each slice into 4 strips.

Makes 12 canapés.

Curried cheese canapés

1 pkg. (3 oz.) cream
    cheese
8 pitted ripe olives,
    chopped
¼ t. curry powder
1 t. chives, chopped
toast rounds

Mix first 4 ingredients. Spread on toast. If desired, add a little lemon juice.

Makes 8–10 canapés.

Hot canapés

Hot canapés may be prepared ahead of time. Simply refrigerate them on the baking or broiling pan, covered, until time to heat and serve.

Cheese and olive canapés

1 c. ripe olives, chopped
½ c. scallions, thinly
  sliced
1½ c. Cheddar cheese,
  grated
½ c. mayonnaise
½ t. salt
½ t. curry powder
toast rounds

Mix all ingredients and spread on toast. Broil until mixture is heated and cheese melted.

Crab meat or lobster canapés

Sprinkle chopped crab or lobster meat with salt, cayenne, and a few drops of lemon juice. Moisten with mayonnaise. Spread on toast rounds. Sprinkle with cheese and brown in oven.

Tuna and cheese canapés

1 c. Cheddar cheese,
    grated
½ c. canned tuna fish
2 T. dry vermouth
black pepper to taste
toast squares

Mix first 4 ingredients. Spread on toast. Bake in a preheated 350° F. oven for 5 min.

Makes 12 canapés.

Deviled sardine canapés

2 T. prepared mustard
juice of 1 lemon
1 can sardines, oil
    reserved
3 T. fine soft bread
    crumbs
4 slices toast, buttered
    and cut into strips the
    size of sardines
lemon wedges,
    watercress, and
    parsley

Mix mustard, lemon juice, and the oil from the can of sardines. Roll sardines in the mixture, then in bread crumbs. Broil for 2–3 min. on both sides. Place on toast strips and anchor with toothpicks. Serve hot on a tray garnished with lemon wedges, watercress, and parsley.

Makes 6 servings.

Sardine canapés

Mash the contents of 2 small cans of sardines. Moisten with a little sardine oil. Add a few drops of lemon juice, Tabasco sauce, and black pepper. Spread on buttered toast fingers. Bake in a preheated 350° F. oven until heated through. Serve with lemon wedges.

Makes 10–12 servings.

Clam and cheese canapés

1 c. Cheddar cheese, grated
1 can (8 oz.) minced clams, drained
pinch of cayenne pepper
2 T. parsley, chopped
1 T. chives, chopped (optional)
toast rounds

Combine first 5 ingredients. Spread on toast rounds. Broil briefly.

Makes 16 canapés.

Sardine and anchovy canapés

1½ t. butter, melted
1 T. anchovy paste
1 T. flour
½ c. white wine
1 can (8 oz.) skinless, boneless sardines
4 slices toast, buttered

Mix butter and anchovy paste until smooth. Add flour, stirring constantly, and cook until mixture bubbles. Gradually add wine, then sardines. Heat slowly. Be careful not to break sardines. Place on toast; add sauce. Serve hot.

Makes 4 servings.

Minced clam canapés

1 large can minced clams, drained
8 oz. cream cheese
2 T. lemon juice
garlic powder to taste
paprika

Mix first 4 ingredients. Spread on toast rounds. Sprinkle with paprika. Toast under broiler until heated and lightly browned.

Parmesan cheese canapés

2 slices bacon
½ c. Parmesan cheese,
  grated
¼ c. evaporated milk
½ t. Worcestershire
  sauce
24 small toast rounds,
  squares, or triangles
pimento-stuffed olives,
  sliced

Cook bacon in a skillet until crisp; crumble. Mix cheese, milk, Worcestershire sauce, and bacon. Spread on toast pieces. Top with olive slices. Bake for 5 min. Serve hot.

Makes 24 canapés.

Preheat oven to 400° F.

Baked cheese canapés

1 pkg. (3 oz.) cream
  cheese
1 t. onions, minced
1 egg, beaten
¼ t. Tabasco sauce
12 toast rounds

Whisk cheese, onions, egg, and Tabasco until light. Spread on toast. Bake until lightly browned.

Makes 12 canapés.

Preheat oven to 375° F.

Tomato, cheese, and anchovy canapés

Spread butter and anchovy paste on toast rounds. Place a thin slice of tomato on top and sprinkle with grated Cheddar cheese. Broil until cheese melts. Serve hot. Garnish with sprigs of parsley or coiled anchovies.

Tomato and cheese canapés

Cut white bread into small rounds with cookie cutter. Toast 1 side and butter the untoasted side. Cut small firm tomatoes into ¼-in. slices. Place tomatoes on buttered side of toast. Season with salt and grated onions. Cover with grated Cheddar cheese. Broil until cheese melts.

Crab and artichoke canapés

½ c. Russian dressing
¼ t. dry mustard
1 can (6 oz.) crab meat,
  picked over well
1 can (10 oz.) artichoke
  bottoms, drained
2 T. parsley, chopped
lemon wedges

Mix dressing and mustard. Fold in crab meat, mixing lightly. Spoon mixture on artichoke bottoms. Just before serving, brown canapés in broiler. Sprinkle with chopped parsley. Garnish with lemon wedges and serve immediately.

Makes 8–10 servings.

Chutney and cheese canapés

Toast rounds of bread on 1 side. Cover the other side with chutney and sprinkle with grated Cheddar cheese. Broil for a few min. until cheese melts. Serve at once.

FREDERICK E. KAHN, M.D. is the general editor for the series of cookbooks to appear under the general title of "Preparing Food the Healthy Way."

Dr. Kahn, a practicing psychiatrist, brings to this series his interest and expertise in the essential nutritional and psychological aspects of personal health. In that vein, he is presently involved in a study of individuals who have suffered from Myocardial Infarction.

He is currently serving as an Assistant Attending Physician at both Columbia College of Physicians and Surgeons, and St. Luke's-Roosevelt Hospital in New York City, and is a member of the Harry Stack Sullivan Society of the William Alanson White Institute for Psychoanalysis.

He is a graduate of the University of Michigan and Wayne State University Medical School.

Index

THE SANDWICH COOKBOOK

PREPARING FOOD THE HEALTHY WAY SERIES
ORDER FORM

If you've enjoyed using this book, and would like copies of any other books in this series, indicate the *number of copies of each title* you wish to order, enclose a check or money order for the appropriate amount, and send in the entire page. Allow 6 weeks for delivery.

NUMBER OF COPIES

____ Appetizers

____ Beverages

____ Breads & Cakes

____ Breakfast & Brunch

____ Canning and Preserving

____ Chinese Food

____ Cooking With Kids

____ Dessert

____ Fish

____ Fruit

NUMBER OF COPIES

____ Ground Meat

____ International Meals

____ One-Dish Meals

____ Outdoor Cooking

____ Party Cooking

____ Poultry

____ Sandwiches

____ Sauces

____ Seafood

Please send me the books checked above. I have ordered ____ books at $4.95 each.

	NUMBER OF COPIES	PER COPY		
	X	$4.95	=	$
Plus postage and handling	X	.50	=	$
Total enclosed				$

Mail this form and your check to: Nautilus Communications, Inc., 460 East 79th Street, New York, NY 10021. No COD's, please!

Name _____

Address _____

City_____ State _____ Zip _____

PREPARING FOOD THE HEALTHY WAY SERIES

ORDER FORM

If you've enjoyed using this book, and would like copies of any other books in this series, indicate the *number of copies of each title* you wish to order, enclose a check or money order for the appropriate amount, and send in the entire page. Allow 6 weeks for delivery.

NUMBER OF COPIES

___ Appetizers
___ Beverages
___ Breads & Cakes
___ Breakfast & Brunch
___ Canning and Preserving
___ Chinese Food
___ Cooking With Kids
___ Dessert
___ Fish
___ Fruit

NUMBER OF COPIES

___ Ground Meat
___ International Meals
___ One-Dish Meals
___ Outdoor Cooking
___ Party Cooking
___ Poultry
___ Sandwiches
___ Sauces
___ Seafood

Please send me the books checked above. I have ordered ___ books at $4.95 each.

	NUMBER OF COPIES	PER COPY		
	X	$4.95	=	$
Plus postage and handling	X	.50	=	$
Total enclosed				$

Mail this form and your check to: Nautilus Communications, Inc., 460 East 79th Street, New York, NY 10021. No COD's, please!

Name _____

Address _____

City _____ State _____ Zip _____